FREE
MONEY
IN AMERICA

RHONDA TURPIN

Other books by Rhonda Turpin

Resilience: Living In Prison with Martha Stewart

Fiction
The Game Is Dead

Look for:
Grant Money in America, Part II of the Money Series

"IF THE MIND CAN CONCEIVE THE ACCOMPLISHMENT, THEN YOU CAN CERTAINLY ACHIEVE IT." My book is to help you get the money.

DISCLAIMER

This publication contains the opinions and ideas of its author, using 30 years of experience. It is sold with the understanding that neither the author nor the publisher is engaged in rendering legal, tax, investment, insurance, financial, accounting, or other professional advice. If the reader requires such advice, a professional should be consulted.

Relevant laws vary from state to state. The strategies outlined in this book has worked well for the author, but may not be suitable for every individual. The author and publisher specifically disclaim any liability of the use and application of the contents of this book.

The names and identifying characteristics of certain individuals referenced in this publication may have been changed.

PUBLISHED BY WORLD BOOKS ETC.

For group discounts of 10 or more, contact World Books Etc., 16781 Chagrin Blvd, Suite 136, Shaker Heights, Ohio 44120.

Cover Design: Jana Rade at www.impactstudiosonline.com
Typesetting/layout: Jana Rade at www.impactstudiosonline.com
Content Editor: Tia Alexa of www.finaltouchhtravel.com

ISBN: 978-0-9821749-0-6

Library of Congress Control Number: 2012935185

Acknowledgments

Extreme Praise to Jehovah God for blessing me with the gift of always thinking outside the stereotype box.

Then, Thanks to my team: Tee and Net, (my daughters), thanks for my "Brady bunch of 3 girls and 3 boys- I have to be very busy at all times(lol); Rick Hagood, the book sales Master, and excellent father to my grandsons; Vanessa Carter, the complimentary side of where I have come from, who I am, and whom I am meant to be; and NEVER least, Floyd Austell, who is rare and cut from the same cloth that I am; WHERE WOULD I BE WITHOUT YOU/MY TEAM? My mind and heart cannot even process that one....

Then to the book scholars: Jana Rade, the fastest and best at what she does; Dezaray Mcmullin, Erika Banks, And Theresa Marchese, my nieces, for your eagerness, questions and comments that help me to keep my skill set sharp; Jamillah Davis, thanks for all the months of being my sounding board; Tia Alexa and Monique Williams, TRUE TO THE GAME New York girls with flavor; Minerva Pascual (Mi-Mi), for constantly expanding my thinking with your analytically mind and creativity on different levels; and Manuelita Buenaflor (Q.P.), for being the perfect librarian and research assistant. Thanks also to the people that have supported my writing, and brought my books.

Join my Facebook family for the latest updates.

Table of Contents

Chapter 1- WHERE IS THE MONEY?   II

Where Does The Money Come from?   12

The Foundation Centers   14

Where Federal money comes from   19

Chapter one-helpful highlights   26

     1. Profiles for three foundations   26

     2. 100 Foundation's assets   36

     3. 25 Foundations that give most   45

     4. 50 Corporate Foundations that give most   48

Chapter 2- WHO GETS THE MONEY?   53

Comparing nonprofits with profit corporations   53

Grants for individuals   55

Difference between profit and nonprofit corps   59

Chapter two-helpful highlights

     sample donor list (also see 6.3)   63

Chapter 3- FREE MONEY QUIZ   65

Intro to the quiz   65

Quiz   66

Evaluation of Skills   67

Chapter 4- HOW DO I GET THE MONEY?   81

Deciding the name of your agency   82
Completing nonprofit articles   91
The EIN form   100
The 1023 application   101
Bylaws; choosing board members   102
Chapter Four-helpful highlights
     Instructions & forms for set up   107

Chapter 5- HOW TO KEEP THE MONEY   123

10 Frequently asked questions   123
10 Components of a grant   125
Chapter five-helpful highlights
Budget Summary   142

Chapter 6- MORE MONEY   147

Car Washes   147
Black Tie Events   149
Annual Campaigns   152
Chapter six-helpful highlights
     1. Annual campaign figures   158
     2. Sample operational budget   159
     3. Sample Donor List (see also 2.2)   160

Chapter 7- MONEY FOR CHURCHES   163

Community Partnerships and Initiatives   167

Role of felons in nonprofits   175

Chapter seven-helpful highlights   179

    1. Characteristics of churches   179

    2. 30 re-entry grantees   180

Chapter 8- MONEY FOR HOUSING   183

Halfway house set-up   183

Funding your halfway house   185

Funding diversity for your halfway house   189

Housing for the elderly   190

Transitional housing   191

Subsidized housing   202

City landbank   211

Chapter eight-helpful highlights   213

    1. HUD news release July 2004   213

    2. HUD news release January 2005   XX

    3. Transitional housing characteristics   XX

    4. Characteristics of Emergency Shelter Grants XX

    5. View of Subsidized Housing   XX

    6. Income Limit Chart   XX

Chapter 9- MONEY FOR DAYCARES 231

Purpose of daycares 231

Types of daycare 232

Set up of daycare programs 232

Diversifying your daycare program 235

Chapter 10- MONEY FOR YOUR STATE 239

The future of nonprofits 239

Chapter ten-helpful highlights 241

nonprofits in 15 selected states 241

GLOSSARY 259

HELPFUL INFORMATION 269

INDEX 271

Chapter 1

Where Is the Money?

Over the past decade, we have been hearing about free money being available to consumers by the billions. Books are advertised regularly. Exciting, fast-talking media bouts lure us to spend a few dollars in order to get the real dollars. There is even a money-back guaranteed clause if a person is not happy with the material in one of the well-known commercials.

I have purchased one of the books advertised twice. The book is true to its guarantee. It does tell you where billions of dollars are in this country. It doesn't explain to you is how to qualify, and access these vast amounts of dollars.

By the time you finish reading this book, you will have a clear understanding on how to access this pool of money. This book is designed to direct you to the money. All you need is the will to follow the suggested steps, and do the work involved. It is free money, you do not have to pay any of it back, but you do have to invest your time and effort.

In order to get paid, you have to understand the process.

WHERE DOES THIS MONEY COME FROM?

After World War II, America attempted to strengthen its economic base, as well as shift the responsibility of taking care of its poor from the government. The government had its hands full, trying to restore the country on its feet. As a result, it was ordered that all profit corporations investing in the stock market would be required to donate a small percentage of their earnings to charity. The purpose of this was to give America a reinvestment plan that was viable. Because of this, thousands of corporations formed foundations to govern the issuance of this money. The foundations were part of the corporation. The corporation provided cash to the nonprofit sector of the business, in order to give it away to charity. The foundation had a separate tax identification number, but often utilized the same corporate staff, and usually had the same chief officers as the profit corporation. The same is true today.

Philanthropy existed in ancient civilizations of the Middle East, Greece, and Rome. Plato's Academy (c. 387 B.C.) established an entity with an endowment that assisted in sustaining the academy's existence for 900 years.

The medieval Christian Church set up a nonprofit foundation to administer money for benevolent purposes.

Even further, the Islamic world entitled an entity as early as the 7th century A.D. in order to support the underprivileged.

The late 19th and 20th centuries witnessed the creation of distinctive large nonprofit organizations and foundations. These large corporations originated out of fortunes of wealthy industrialists.

Listed below are examples, with a few foundation assets and giving amounts. They are listed by the name of the foundation first, with the founder name following when noted. The last item listed is the date the foundation was formed. Remember this is a small list of some of the most popular foundations that still give away millions of dollars to date.

Foundation	Founder	Year
The Smithsonian Institution	James Smithson	1847
Peabody Education Fund	George Peabody	1867
The Carnegie Foundation	Andrew Carnegie	1905
The Rockefeller Foundation	John D. Rockefeller	1913
Russell Saga Foundation		1907
The Commonwealth Fund		1918
John Simon Guggenheim Memorial Foundation		1925
The Ford Foundation		1936
W.K. Kellogg Foundation		1930
The Robert Wood Johnson Foundation		1936
The Pew Memorial Trust		1948
John D. and Katherine T. MacArthur Foundation		1970

The Above Foundations comprise some of the grandfathers of grant-giving. Billions of accumulated dollars have been given away over five generations. There are thousands of foundations in America.

THE FOUNDATIONS CENTERS

With the boom of new foundations in the decade ranging from 1936 to 1946, after the War, there needed to be a central way to attempt to centralize data and information. This was done through a donor by way of a grant. A non- profit agency was set up for this specific purpose. The agency was named *The Foundation Center*. It was formed in 1957. No other place in the world can answer better the question of "Where is the money?" than the Foundation Centers throughout the country. The Foundation Centers are there to assist individuals working for and affiliated with nonprofits with the research of finding funding sources, and beginning their rules and guidelines for accessing funds.

The Foundation Center is not all inclusive on listing agencies giving to charity. Some Corporations wish to remain private, but give out large sums of money to worthy causes, such as cancer research or stem cell research. The money given away is the corporation's hard earned profits. They can give it away as they see fit to any project that qualifies under "underserved, or underprivileged." The minimum amount of money given away annually is decided by the chosen board members of the foundation, and heads of the corporation. As I stated, it is one of the same. There is no written rule that states the President of the Rockefeller Corporation cannot also be the President of the nonprofit foundation.

There are three main Foundation Centers spanning across the United States. They are located in Ohio, New York, and California. The central office is located in Ohio in downtown Cleveland, inside the Hanna Building, across from Playhouse Square. I have frequented this particular office so much that during some of my gorilla research spells, I have been recognized and addressed by name. The staff is helpful and polite, and they do have free fresh- brewed coffee for coffee lovers like me. Also it is important to note that the coffee is free. I usually accept with gratitude.

In order to get the most benefits from the Foundation Center, when you enter, you should already have a general idea of the type of project that you are looking to fund. The second thing you should have a general idea about is the approximate figure that you are looking for to fund the project. The

reason why this is important is because if you are looking to fund a million dollar project, you will need to complete a lot more research than if you were looking to obtain a small amount of money for a neighborhood project.

For example, I headed out to the Foundation Center one morning to attempt to obtain $5000 for a high school band project, that would pay for the band having new matching, colorful uniforms. The grant was in partnership with one of the neighborhood development corporations that held most of their events at the high school auditorium. This was an easy project. Within the hour, I had researched five local foundations that gave away grant awards of $5000 quarterly. For the small amount, they did not list the need to wait for a full board presentation. The money was able to be approved by contacting one of the board members anytime, and arranging whatever documentation they requested. Finding a small amount of money like $5000 did not take a lot of time or research. In fact, at the end of the day, I had a choice of whom I was going to ask for the money, and more than one willing funder. You can only pick one. To pick more than one, for the same amount of money, would be illegal and what is called double dipping.

To research a grant for large amounts of money, expect to spend a few hours minimum. Your time will be used scanning through the database of potential funders. Write down their restrictions to the grant, and the previous amounts rewarded to agencies similar to yours in service delivery, so you will not ask for too much more than what a foundation normally gives per quarter.

You do not need money when visiting the Foundation Center. It is a nonprofit, and is free of charge. What you do need is a pen or pencil, a notebook or some writing paper in order to keep the researched data in some kind of accessible order for future reference, and most of all, patience and willing-ness to sit down and find the money. No degrees, certifications, or special training is needed.

When visiting the Foundation Center, always allow yourself a few hours. If you rush, you may miss some dollars. I have more than once dashed in and out to research a particular foundation, only to find out a week later that the Foundation Center had information of a new foundation giving out ten times more money quarterly.

The center has library books that are to be used as reference, and also a large amount of books that are for sale covering a wide array of subjects. It has an up-to-date database so that you can access funding sources by the name of the foundation, or the area you are looking to fund. For example, if you are looking to fund an adult education program, you can reference foundations that fund that sort of project. They also offer a database of corporation filings that will allow you to view a foundation's assets, and also for some foundations, whom and where they gave to over a period of a few years. This can be also helpful in deciding how much money to ask a particular foundation for.

Last, but also important is the Foundation Center website. You can bring the entire list of funders into your living room by visiting their website. Their website also has a calendar of events. They offer free workshops on many topics spanning from how to access grant money, to how to use the library to achieve the most benefit. It is totally free, and advertised in advance on the calendar. The workshops are on a first- come first- serve basis. There are a few workshops that may cost, but I do not remember ever having to pay anything. Also, there may be some foundations that you may not be able to access by internet. You may have to visit the Foundation library in person. Not all foundations giving away money have a website. In addition, you can subscribe to their free weekly newsletter that will give you a list of available funding, its minimum criteria, and the deadlines for submitting your grant. Where is the money? You can definitely find it at the Foundation Centers. For cities not listed as major offices, The Foundation Centers has annexes all over the country. They are usually placed in universities. Those are just as helpful. Internet access is the first step to tapping into finding sources if you live in a town where it requires a lot of driving to get to the nearest University offering a Foundation Center Annex.

The following will give you the website, the three main centers strategically placed throughout the United States, and the necessary phone numbers. With the information below, using computer, telephone, or a letter, you will be able to contact the Foundation Center successfully.

There are also hundreds of pay sites that will give you funding information. I have never subscribed, so I cannot give an honest opinion of any of them.

WHERE FEDERAL MONEY COMES FROM

The second major place where the money is, is in your possession at least temporarily. When tax season comes around every year, you pass it on to Internal Revenue Service, who in turn passes it on to the President. The President then passes it on to charity.

The President of the United States has 13 cabinets. They are listed below:

1. Department of Transportation
2. Secretary of State
3. Department of Treasury

4. Department of Defense
5. Department of Interior
6. Department of Commerce
7. Department of Veteran's Affairs
8. Department of Energy
9. Department of Health and human Services
10. Department of Agriculture
11. Department of Housing and Urban Development
12. Department of Labor
13. Department of Education

Only the last seven of these cabinets offer grants to agencies, with the three most common being the Department of Health and Human Services, The Department of Housing and Urban Development, and the Department of Education. The rest of the departments may have an initiative every once in a while, but it is not common.

When the government gives away money, a large percentage of the money comes from taxes. There are five areas that are taxed in order to provide a source of revenue for the federal government. They are:

1. Personal income taxes
2. Corporate/payroll taxes
3. Excise taxes (alcohol, gas, tobacco)
4. Social insurance taxes and contributions
5. Estate and gift taxes

Of the above, personal income taxes provide the federal government with the largest amount of revenue.

The president decides the budget yearly. Also at this time, He also decides out of the 13 agencies, what amounts will be awarded, or what percentage of revenues will be given out. It's all about how big a slice of the pie that the President determines each one gets.

For example, former President John F. Kennedy decided that he would tackle the disparities among housing throughout the United States. There had been a fair housing act passed after World War II, but it was never enforced until President Kennedy decided to enforce it.

I do not remember former President Kennedy's platform for fair-housing. However, I do remember well former President Clinton's Welfare-to-Work campaign. I had already began my profession as a part-time grantwriter and consultant, and had to explain several times that the focus was no longer on Drug Treatment or anything else, but welfare-to-work. If an agency had a good job readiness or training component, they were able to access funding without much of a problem. The compassion for drug treatment programs however, diminished. Funding was cut tremendously in the area of drug rehabilitation. Some drug programs were forced to go out of business. Legislators made it clear that the focus had changed. Another one of former President Clinton's focuses at the end of his term was the Youth Development Initiative. Mentoring and After-School programs were set up all over the country with the designated funding. I was able to set up three sites myself, with the agency's summer camp program rated the fourth in the country.

President Bush rallied the Faith-Based Initiative. He insisted on federal funding trickling down to agencies that had a holistic component, including some spirituality. What that did was open the door for more churches to set up nonprofit organizations and be able to access funding. However, some Foundations like the Cleveland Foundation, a community foundation located in Cleveland, Ohio, always gave to faith-based organizations, therefore they did not have to alter their focus. Steve Rowen was the program officer for the faith-based initiative funding, and encouraged holistic approaches in service delivery for all agencies, not just churches and faith-based agencies.

What occurs is once the President delegates the funding agency that will govern a certain amount of dollars, the chosen agency then picks a state or county agency to accept proposals, and monitor the programs and spending. It could be the county commissioners' office or the county department of health or human services for example. It could also be the state department of Education, if the Federal Department of Education is the recipient of the funding.

How the states and counties are chosen to receive the funding is by information gathered through census studies as well as other data and statistics. An example of this was when eight counties were awarded the largest amount of the Youth Development Initiative grant. The reason these counties were chosen was because of the Department of Justice statistics depicting that children got into trouble between the hours of 3 and 7pm, Monday through Friday. The counties that received the largest bulk of money had a high number of crime committed by children during those hours. The initiative was set up in order to combat and decrease crime committed during these hours. This is how an Initiative from the President's office works. For the Youth Development Initiative, Cuyahoga County was given $129 million. It is wise to assume that the entire country received around eight billion, minimum. A few other targeted cities were New York, and Chicago.

Cuyahoga County received the funds through the County Department of Justice Affairs. The first round went through the Department of Health and Human Services, and did not reach the office of Juvenile Justice until well into the second round. Why? Some of the funding Initiatives are very political. In my opinion, someone made someone angry and the changing of the guard took place. It happens all the time in the large administrative offices.

I was part of the Youth Development Initiative. I attended the original RFP (Request for Proposal) meeting. I also assisted in forming a ten agency collaboration for the southeast side of Cleveland. The orders came from the County Commissioners. They wanted to make sure that the collaboration was a well-rounded group, and that small grass root agencies were included. I wrote the grant with Paula Mayes, Executive Director of Garfield

Heights Community Center. We worked around the clock to put together the collaboration, and to write the grant. Ms. Mayes' agency became the fiscal manager of the grant. My agency became the program manager. Both tasks were a large responsibility. Ms. Mayes was responsible for doing all of the accounting and fiscal reporting to the county commissioners. She was also responsible for pulling some of the smaller agencies up to par. I collected the program reports from all ten agencies annually, and compiled them into one large report to turn into the County Commissioners. I worked closely with their program officer, Sheila Turner, while Mrs. Mayes worked closely with the County's fiscal officer. The amount of the grant was for five million dollars. Despite the challenges, the project went well. Our collaboration easily served over 1300 families with a wide array of services ranging from field trips to horse training as therapy.

Another example of how an initiative works was the Literacy Initiative. The Department of Education was awarded a large sum of funding in order to address the large percentages of illiterate Americans. The U.S. Department of Education passed the money down to the State Department, and the State Department was the recipient of the award to distribute to the agencies that were eligible. Also they offered an on-going component where you could have your employee certified as a tutor, and then bill them continuously for tutoring hours if your employee was state certified. Literacy Centers were formed in the inner city, to make the locations more accessible for people without transportation. It is a very good program. Some of the best programs in the world were formed as a result of an initiative.

Scholarships also fall under grants, and are often given away by private corporations. Scholarships are like grants in that you do not have to pay them back. However, you do have to usually keep a certain grade point average, and remain in school. Usually scholarships have a time limit also. The common time limit is four years, but I have known students to receive scholarships on a one-time only basis. Fellowships are a lot of the same.

So where is the Money? To sum it up, the money is in corporations that set up foundations or give to charity, and as part of the tax base in America that the President rules. The latter is your county block grants that funnel through county agencies, state grants, and federal government agencies such as HUD. The Department of Energy gives agencies like HEAP (Housing Energy Assistance Program, funding to pass out to communities and neighborhoods.

Chapter 1: Helpful Highlights 1:

Corporations give to satisfy a legal requirement, and to be in compliance and reap all of the tax benefits from being in compliance. The U.S. government demands a payout requirement of large corporations. Corporations have a legal obligation to disburse annually approximately 5 percent of the value of the investment portfolio. This funding is controlled by the trustees. Foundations can pay out more than 5 percent if they choose to.

The Internal Revenue Code requires private foundations to annually pay 2 percent of net investment income, defined as interest. When a corporation gives 5%, the federal excise tax is included in this amount. The payout requirement is satisfied by payments for grants, and other characteristic activities.

The following information gives the reader a summary of three large foundations in order to clarify where the money is, and where it comes from. The following information are the questions that need to be addressed:

1. Contact Information
2. Type of Foundation
3. Assets
4. Total Giving
5. Primary funding areas

The Ford Family Foundation
100 Wall St., 11th Floor
New York, NY 10005

Henry Ford and his son, Edsel, established the foundation in 1936, in Michigan, through several gifts of Ford Motor Stock. Since 1936, the Ford Foundation has made more than $12.5 billion in grants. In the period following World War ll, Ford was the largest foundation in the United States.

The Ford Foundation is an independent foundation, with total assets for 2005 listed as $19,671,879. Total giving for 2005 was $581,018. For more than 5 decades the foundation focuses its grant making into three program areas.

1. Assets Building & Community
    Development
2. Peace & Social Justice, and Knowledge,
    Creativity & Freedom

Ford has a global presence and believes in the value of linking grantees in one part of the world with those elsewhere. Coming together builds understanding of approaches that work and enables the spread of best practices. Ford grant making incorporates opportunities for grantees to observe each others work up close, to meet in conference or to create web sites and other tools that foster the exchange of ideas and the development of relationships across communities and continents.

Grants to the Ford Foundation for under $200,000 can be approved locally. Check the Ford Foundation web site to get a full list of the office locations in the U.S. Grant request for over $200,000 are considered at the main office only in New York. The New York staff meets bi-weekly to review grant applications. Each year Ford receives about 40,000 proposals and makes 2,000 grants. Requests range from a few thousand dollars to millions of dollars and are accepted in categories such as planning grants, project support, general support, and endowments. There are no application deadlines. Requests are considered throughout the year. Instead of sending in the entire grant proposal, the staff recommends that applicants first send in a brief letter of inquiry. The letter should include:

1. The purpose of the project
2. The problems and issues to be addressed
3. Information about the organization
4. An estimated overall project budget
5. The period of time the funds would cover
6. The qualifications of those engaged in the project

In response, if interested in the project, Ford Foundation staff may ask for a formal proposal. Formal proposals include:

1. A description of the proposed work and how it will be conducted
2. The names and biographies of those engaged in the project
3. The organizations current budget
4. A detailed project budget
5. The organizations current means of support and the status of its applications to other funding sources
6. The organizations legal and tax status

Ford usually allocates grants covering a two year budget period. Staff is encouraged to make plans for 65 percent of their budget allocation, leaving 35 percent free for unforeseen opportunities. The foundation has a long-term focus, and does renew grants to organizations that demonstrate that they are making progress toward their objectives.

In reviewing proposals, grant makers look for fresh thinking people and organizations that are effective and collaborative, and evidence that the proposed project helps fulfill the foundations mission. Applicants can expect a response within six weeks whether their proposals are within the foundations program interests and are being seriously considered for funding.

Ford makes grants to individuals limited to research, training and travel directly related to our program interests. These grants are awarded through publicly announced competitions or on the basis of nominations from universities and other nonprofit institutions. Often, Ford hires evaluators to help monitor groups of grants or a single grantee's work.

In 2005, Ford distributed $622 million, exceeding the federal mandated payout by $79 million. During the past five years, the foundation has made $3.4 billion in qualifying distributions, exceeding the federally mandated payout requirement by $625 million.

The second Foundation to give a glimpse of is the Rockefeller Foundation.

The Rockefeller Foundation
420 5th Avenue
New York, NY 10018-2702
Telephone: (212) 869-8500
www.rockfound.org

The Rockefeller Foundation is an independent foundation with total assets for 2005 listed as $3,417,557,613. Total giving for 2005 was $222,083,354. The three areas where funding is directed is:

1. Environmental quality
2. Equal opportunity for all
3. Cultural development with emphasis in drama, literature and music

The foundation was established by John D. Rockefeller Sr. on May 14, 1913. It was one of the first philanthropies to operate on a worldwide basis, addressing hunger problems on an international level. John D. Rockefeller received his fortune from his invention of the modern petroleum industry, and also pioneered the forces that modernized American medical science. Rockefeller originally endowed the foundation with $100 million. He later increased his endowment amount to $183 million. Today the foundations endowment is estimated to be between $700 and $800 million.

Rockefeller does not specialize in research grants. It funds and conducts its own research through Rockefeller University, previously named the Rockefeller Institution for Medical Research.

After World War 1, the Rockefeller Center was established in New York as one of the most important tourist attractions in the city, and the symbol of 20th century urbanism. The structure is 70 stories high and 18 buildings of consortium. Each of the centers original structures were planned in relation to one another to maximize use of available space and air, and a network of underground loading docks was built to minimize the truck traffic. The complex has offices, shops, restaurants, NBC studios, Associated Press, Simon & Schuster buildings, Radio City Music Hall and General Electric.

Below is an example of grants awarded by the Rockefeller Foundation during April and May of

2007, to give the reader an example of amounts and types of grants awarded.

Name	Approved date	Amount
1.) Ministry of Women's Affairs Phnom Penh Cambodia	5/16/2007	$150,000
For continued support of women's vulnerability to HIV/AIDS.		
2.) Institute of Development Studies Brighton England	5/16/2007	$134,842
To promote an integrated climate change resilience program in South Asia.		
3.) Stanford University Stanford CA United States	5/16/2007	$40,000
In support of travel costs for conference on climate change		
4.) Enterprise Louisiana Loan Fund, LLC	5/8/2007	$1,000,000
To assist in rebuilding housing for low-income residents after hurricane Katrina.		
5.) Eva Quintana Mourelle Barcelona Spain	4/27/2007	$11,200
To assist in development of an evaluation plan for climate change resilience initiative.		
6.) Global Alliance for TB Drug Development New York, NY United States	4/23/2007	$100,000
To assist in development of affordable tuberculosis drugs in developing countries.		

Name	Approved date	Amount
7). International Health Policy Program Nonthaburi Thailand Toward the costs of a study to evaluate pandemic influenza.	4/19/2007	$63,720
8). Agricultural College San Jose Costa Rica In support of the participation of African scholars for Global conference.	4/11/2007	$25,000
9). Rodolfo Morales Cultural Foundation Oaxaca Mexico Toward cost of completing artist work on the phenomenon of migration in the U.S. and Mexico.	4/11/2007	$80,000

From studying recent grant awards of the Rockefeller Foundation it shows that they are highly interested in climate change resilience, and on an international level at this time. By studying annual reports and grant awards of other foundations, you can get a feel for their priorities and award amounts.

The third foundation to be summarized is W.K. Kellogg Foundation.

The W.K. Kellogg Foundation www.wkkf.org

The Kellogg Foundation is an independent foundation with total assets for 2006 listed as $7.8 billion. Total giving for 2006 was $329 million.

The company was founded in 1900 by W.K. Kellogg and his brother, Dr. John H. Kellogg, who together developed a method of producing crunchy, flavorful flakes that proved a popular breakfast food among the patients at Dr. Kellogg's hospital. A serious marketing plan was implemented. The company prospered quickly. W.K. Kellogg bought his brother out, and put $45 million donation into the foundation in 1930. The Kellogg Foundation supports a social improvement and child welfare. Kellogg has built a bird sanctuary, schools, and a youth center for Michigan residents.

Kellogg Foundation also provides start-up money to organizations and institutions for specific projects, mainly in the United States, Latin America and southern Africa. The Foundation appropriated $39 million of immediate relief and on-going support to organizations working on the ground in the Gulf Coast region in the aftermath of Hurricane Katrina.

The foundation does not support research projects or make grants to individuals.

In summing up three large foundations that are considered to be the grandfathers of philanthropy, the information presents a general foundation and standard for all foundations.

Chapter 1: Helpful Highlights 2:

Below are the top 100 largest grantmaking foundations ranked by their assets:

Rank	Name	State	Assets	Year
1.	Bill & Melinda Gates Foundation	WA	$33,120,381,000	2006
2.	The Ford Foundation	NY	12,252,645,528	2006
3.	Paul Getty Trust	CA	10,133,371,844	2006
4.	The Robert Wood Johnson Foundation	NJ	9,367,614,774	2005
5.	The William and Flora Hewlett Foundation	CA	8,520,764,000	2006
6.	W.K. Kellogg Foundation	MI	7,799,270,734	2006
7.	Lily Endowment Inc.	IN	7,601,664,181	2006
8.	The David and Lucille Packard Foundation	CA	6,350,664,410	2006
9.	The Andrew W. Mellion Foundation	NY	6,130,848,000	2006
10.	John D. and Catherine T. MacArthur Foundation	IL	5,492,269,240	2005
11.	Gordon and Betty Moore Foundation	CA	5,308,627,945	2005
12.	The California Endowment	CA	4,405,938,934	2005
13.	The Rockefeller Foundation	NY	3,417,557,613	2005
14.	The Starr Foundation	NY	3,344,801,753	2005
15.	The Annie E. Casey	MD	3,265,655,271	2006
16.	The Kresge Foundation	MI	3,032,422,497	2005
17.	The Duke Endowment	NC	2,708,834,085	2005

Rank	Name	State	Assets	Year
18.	Charles Stewart Mott Foundation	MI	2,629,297,078	2006
19.	The Annenberg Foundation	PA	2,539,268,854	2006
20.	Carnegie Corporation of New York	NY	2,530,191,576	2006
21.	John S. and James L. Knight Foundation	FL	2,342,624,401	2006
22.	Casey Family Programs	WA	2,265,711,291	2005
23.	Tulsa Community Foundation	OK	2,264,564,027	2005
24.	Robert W. Woodruff Foundation	GA	2,250,689,422	2006
25.	The McKnight Foundation	MN	2,213,868,000	2006
26.	The Harry and Jeanette Weinberg Foundation	MD	2,154,005,108	2006
27.	Richard King Melion Foundation	PA	2,088,186,647	2006
28.	Ewing Marion Kaufmann Foundation	MO	2,067,471,575	2006
29.	The New York Community Trust	NY	2,042,798,738	2006
30.	Doris Duke Charitable Foundation	NY	1,920,145,122	2005
31.	The Cleveland Foundation	OH	1,889,098,831	2006
32.	Broad Foundation	CA	1,802,485,000	2006
33.	The James Irvin Foundation	CA	1,610,480,320	2006
34.	The Wallace Foundation	NY	1,586,977,058	2006
35.	Alfred P. Sloan Foundation	NY	1,581,350,875	2005
36.	The Chicago Community Trust	IL	1,503,994,247	2005
37.	The William Penn Foundation	PA	1,428,365,937	2006
38.	W.M. Keck Foundation	CA	1,410,261,448	2006

Rank	Name	State	Assets	Year
39.	Lumina Foundation for Education, Inc.	IN	1,363,176,000	2006
40.	Houston Endowment, Inc.	TX	1,338,767,885	2006
41.	The Samuel Roberts Noble Foundation	OK	1,337,857,120	2006
42.	Walton Family Foundation, Inc.	AR	1,328,793,250	2005
43.	The California Wellness Foundation	CA	1,301,438,867	2006
44.	The Michael and Susan Dell Foundation	TX	1,226,020,349	2005
45.	The Brown Foundation, Inc.	TX	1,223,019,722	2006
46.	Kimbell Art Foundation	TX	1,210,790,189	2005
47.	Daniels Fund	CO	1,185,701,276	2006
48.	Donald W. Reynolds Foundation	NV	1,181,839,935	2006
49.	The Moody Foundation	TX	1,158,543,467	2005
50.	California Community Foundation	CA	1,152,601,808	2006
51.	Marin Community Foundation	CA	1,125,930,427	2006
52.	Freeman Foundation	NY	1,105,466,120	2005
53.	John Templeton Foundation	PA	1,080,335,362	2005
54.	The Freedom Forum, Inc.	VA	1,071,127,819	2005
55.	The Ahmanson Foundation	CA	1,036,120,000	2006
56.	Greater Kansas City Community Foundation	MO	1,013,035,000	2005
57.	The Oregon Community Foundation	OR	996,491,247	2006
58.	The Joyce Foundation	IL	975,275,000	2006
59.	The Meadows Foundation	TX	974,254,634	2006

Rank	Name	State	Assets	Year
60.	The Saint Paul Foundation	MN	909,500,000	2006
61.	Conrad N. Hilton Foundation	NV	889,768,444	2006
62.	The San Francisco Foundation	CA	883,443,000	2006
63.	Hall Family Foundation	MO	883,436,222	2006
64.	Bush Foundation	MN	873,280,162	2006
65.	Surdna Foundation, Inc	NY	859,153,983	2006
66.	The Packard Humanities Institute	CA	858,955,029	2005
67.	Open Society Institute	NY	858,935,162	2005
68.	Bart Foundation	MA	857,054,761	2005
69.	The Columbus Foundation and Affiliated Organizations	OH	850,089,853	2005
70.	The Edna McConnell Clark Foundation	NY	846,456,297	2006
71.	Weingart Foundation	CA	839,604,507	2006
72.	Rockefeller Brothers Fund, Inc	NY	815,561,407	2005
73.	Longwood Foundation	DE	795,205,527	2006
74.	The Henry Luce Foundation, Inc.	NY	792,916,471	2005
75.	Burroughs Welicome Fund	NC	777,620,142	2006
76.	The J.E. and L.E. Mabee Foundation, Inc.	OK	769,999,802	2006
77.	Boston Foundation, Inc.	MA	769,807,869	2006
78.	Community Foundation Silicon Valley	CA	760,821,244	2005
79.	M. J. Murdock Charitable Trust	WA	758,617,116	2005
80.	Fred C. Katherine B. Andersen Foundation	MN	752,341,252	2005
81.	The Pittsburgh Foundation	PA	742,455,439	2006

Rank	Name	State	Assets	Year
82.	Hartford Foundation for Public Giving	CT	735,105,228	2006
83.	Marguerite Casey Foundation	WA	719,973,982	2006
84.	The Lynde and Harry Bradley Foundation, Inc.	WI	706,076,838	2005
85.	The Commonwealth Fund	NY	701,275,427	2006
86.	Communities Foundation of Texas, Inc.	TX	699,873,000	2006
87.	The AVI CHAI Foundation	NY	688,392,372	2006
88.	The Picower Foundation	FL	685,672,092	2006
89.	The John A. Hartford Foundation, Inc.	NY	679,770,507	2005
90.	Robertson Foundation	NY	659,047,413	2005
91.	The Minneapolis Foundation	MN	654,649,964	2006
92.	Community Foundation for Greater Atlanta, Inc.	GA	638,817,268	2006
93.	John Kent Cooke Foundation	VA	637,795,172	2006
94.	Leon Levy Foundation	NY	628,514,927	2006
95.	Publix Super Markets Charities	FL	625,587,255	2006
96.	The Robert A. Welch Foundation	TX	625,127,762	2006
97.	William Randolph Hearst Foundation	NY	624,489,259	2005
98.	The Virginia G. Piper Charitable Trust	AZ	615,668,089	2006
99.	Peninsula Community Foundation	CA	614,336,446	2005
100.	Wayne & Gladys Valley Foundation	CA	607,517,865	2006

Chapter 1: Helpful Highlights 3:

This section will inform the reader of the 25 largest community foundations who give out the most money. You will note that the Foundations that have the most assets from the top 100 list we gave do not necessarily give out the most money.

Rank	Name	State	Total Giving	Year
1.	The New York Community Trust	NY	$157,444,070	2006
2.	Greater Kansas City Community Foundation	MO	140,702,000	2005
3.	Greater Houston Community Foundation	TX	20 109,144,475 05	2005
4.	Peninsula Community Foundation	CA	92,331,777	2005
5.	California Community Foundation	CA	91,367,805	2006
6.	The Community Foundation for the National Capital Region	DC	91,235,382	2006
7.	Community Foundation for Greater Atlanta, Inc.	GA	89,391,237	2006
8.	The Chicago Community Trust	IL	75,988,536	2005
9.	Community Foundation Silicon Valley	CA	75,366,593	2005
10.	The Cleveland Foundation	OH	72,148,229	2006
11.	The San Francisco Foundation	CA	68,100,000	2006
12.	The Columbus Foundation	OH	65,626,215	2005

Rank	Name	State	Total Giving	Year
13.	Boston Foundation, Inc.	MA	60,811,605	2006
14.	Communities Foundation of Texas, Inc	TX	59,931,000	2006
15.	Foundation for the Carolinas	NC	59,551,103	2005
16.	Omaha Community Foundation	NE	53,598,735	2005
17.	Marin Community Foundation	CA	51,649,386	2005
18.	The Seattle Foundation	WA	45,948,620	2005
19.	Community Foundation of Northwest Indiana, Inc.	IN	44,206,544	2005
20.	The San Diego Foundation	CA	43,192,006	2006
21.	The Oregon Community Foundation	OR	43,197,006	2006
22.	The Minneapolis Foundation	MN	37,154,937	2006
23.	The Pittsburgh Foundation	PA	33,930,106	2006
24.	The Dayton Foundation	OH	33,858,562	2006
25.	Community Foundation for Southeast Michigan	MI	33,600,467	2006

Chapter I: Helpful Highlights 4:

This section lists the 50 largest corporate foundations ranked by total giving. When you are seeking out the money, always see if a corporation has a charitable foundation set up. Be sure to learn about the Corporation, its product, and the mission statement of the corporation before attempting to apply for grant money from them.

Rank	Name	State	Total Giving	Year
1.	Averts Pharmaceuticals Health Care Foundation	NJ	$217,845,821	2005
2.	Wal-Mart Foundation	AR	155,073,615	2006
3.	The Bank of America Charitable Foundation, Inc.	NC	123,287,818	2005
4.	The JP Morgan Chase Foundation	NY	84,516,858	2005
5.	Ford Motor Company Fund	MI	79,881,090	2005
6.	GE Foundation	CT	70,635,496	2005
7.	The Wells Fargo Foundation	CA	64,359,430	2006
8.	Johnson & Johnson Family of Companies Contribution Fund	NJ	62,563,309	2005
9.	ExxonMobil Foundation	TX	62,495,330	2006
10.	Verizon Foundation	NJ	61,834,820	2005
11.	The Wachovia Foundation, Inc	NC	57,363,628	2005
12.	AT&T Foundation	TX	47,556,509	2005
13.	Intel Foundation	OR	43,102,949	2005
14.	The Merck Company Foundation	NJ	41,596,595	2005
15.	The UPS Foundation	GA	39,694,742	2005

Rank	Name	State	Total Giving	Year
16.	General Motors Foundation, Inc.	MI	39,338,242	2005
17.	BP Foundation, Inc.	IL	35,500,792	2005
18.	MetLife Foundation	NY	31,999,651	2005
19.	Eli Lilly and Company Foundation	IN	26,799,878	2005
20.	Abbot Laboratories Fund	IL	26,217,474	2005
21.	The Prudential Foundation	NJ	26,018,724	2005
22.	The Procter & Gamble Fund	OH	25,009,145	2006
23.	NCC Charitable Foundation	OH	24,868,048	2006
24.	The HCA Foundation	TN	23,934,875	2005
25.	Caterpillar Foundation	IL	23,914,262	2005
26.	The Coca-Cola Foundation	GA	23,912,780	2005
27.	The Bristol-Myers Squibb Foundation	NY	23,009,102	2005
28.	The Pfizer Foundation	NY	22,874,796	2005
29.	The PepsiCo Foundation	NY	22,789,562	2006
30.	Alcoa Foundation	PA	22,749,270	2005
31.	Freddi Mac Foundation	VA	22,539,727	2006
32.	Blue Shield of California Foundation	CA	21,706,334	2005
33.	Daimier Chrysler Corporation Fund	MI	21,245,642	2006
34.	Merrill Lynch & Co. Foundation, Inc.	NY	21,225,243	2005
35.	The Capital Group Companies Charitable Foundation	CA	20,600,732	2006
36.	The Medtronic Foundation	MN	20,409,562	2006
37.	U.S. Bancorp Foundation, Inc.	MN	20,271,339	2005

Rank	Name	State	Total Giving	Year
38.	General Mills Foundation	MN	20,200,005	2006
39.	State Farm Companies Foundation	IL	19,802,268	2006
40.	American Express Foundation	NY	19,693,310	2005
41.	3M Foundation	MN	19,587,243	2005
42.	Emerson Charitable Trust	MO	19,415,009	2005
43.	New York Life Foundation	NY	18,120,471	2006
44.	The Allstate Foundation	IL	17,564,554	2006
45.	Amgen Foundation, Inc	CA	16,541,439	2005
46.	Simpson PSB Fund	CA	16,075,734	2005
47.	The Dow Chemical Company Foundation	MI	15,953,729	2005
48.	Duke Energy Foundation	NC	15,481,432	2005
49.	Deutsche Bank Americas Foundation	NY	15,052,749	2005
50.	Nationwide Foundation	OH	14,863,457	2005

Chapter 2

Who Gets
The Money?

Who gets the money is nonprofit organizations, and in rare cases, individuals. In order to receive grant money, you have to be a nonprofit, 501-C-3 agency. Many people get grants and loans confused. There are many low-interest loans that are available; however, a loan is not a grant. You may pay it back, no matter how low the interest-rate that the lender gives you.

A nonprofit organization or agency is set up in order to provide services to the community or group of people that it wants to serve. This is usually listed on the state and federal forms for setting up a nonprofit, to be discussed in detail in the following chapter.

COMPARING NONPROFIT
WITH PROFIT CORPORATIONS

A nonprofit does not mean that you cannot make money. In contrast, the executive directors and managers of some of the larger nonprofit national agencies such as United

Way, Red Cross, and the Boys and Girls Club reach well into the middle six-figure range. I have witnessed nonprofit salaries running neck-to-neck with profit corporations. The only difference has been the customer base. That is strictly a myth that nonprofit directors don't make a profit, or don't get paid well. The term nonprofits came from the general rule of the corporation structuring. According to the Internal Revenue Service, every dollar that you get into the agency must be spent on the agency mission and expenses.

For example, if you receive a grant for a million dollars, you cannot treat the money like you have won the lotto. You cannot buy that new car that you have been wanting for the past decade. You can't buy the mother-in-law a new house to get her out of yours, or even the wife that new mink sable coat that she wants. Nope. You cannot use agency money for personal use. However, that is really not much different that the rule of a profit corporation.

If you are receiving a salary from a profit corporation, you cannot take any payments coming in and buy personal items. You can use your salary to buy whatever you want if you can afford it. If you can't, you cannot use customer payments as they come in just because you are an employee of the corporation. Have you ever heard of the words stealing, embezzlement, fraud, or prison? If you take customer payments off the top, outside of your salary, or you spend funder's grant money for your personal use, outside of your paycheck, you will eventually become very familiar with the mentioned negative terms. If you receive a grant for $100,000, and your salary is only $10,000 of that award, you must not touch the other $90,000. It belongs strictly to the organization to accomplish its mission, to the community. If you want to take your paycheck or part of the grant and spend it on whatever you want, it is legally allowed, just as you take your paycheck in a profit business.

If a grant says that the agency is supposed to provide free lunch to 70 kids for the summer for $90,000, the services need to be provided and documented by the use of sign-in sheets.

GRANTS FOR INDIVIDUALS

One of the most commonly asked questions that is asked is, "Can I receive a grant?" The answer is no. Grants are not generally given to individuals. The exception is an educational grant for school, such as a Pell Grant, or state grant. These types of grants are given to individuals in order to assist the student with tuition and other costs relating to attending college. These individual grants have to be applied for. They are usually applied for through the financial aid office of the college or university. Now libraries offer the financial aid applications in most states.

These individual grants follow the same guidelines that other grants follow. You have to meet the requirements by fitting into the income guidelines. Most grants are set up to serve the underprivileged or disadvantaged. College assistance grants are no different.

The college educational grants are issued generally to the financial aid office of the college. The college will deduct the tuition, and then issue a check for the balance of the grant to the student in order to assist with books and supplies if there is anything left. Sometimes there is nothing left over. A student may even need to add money to the grant in order to cover tuition. Financial aid advisors or counselors will be able to assist a student with applying for grants, if income eligible.

The usual term that you can receive grants is a limit of four years. If you do not achieve a degree within the allotted amount of time, you are no longer eligible in most states to continue to receive assistance. Because it is a grant, you do NOT have to pay back the money, once allotted.

College grants are a common type of grant.

As stated in the previous chapter, scholarships are also given to individuals. Fellowships are also. Scholarships and Fellowships are not income specific. Your parents can be rich, and you can still receive a scholarship or fellowship if your grades and focus meet the guidelines. The reason for that is because Scholarships and Fellowships are given away from corporations and foundations. Some of the foundations were set up specifically to give away scholarships. Foundations and corporations are not governed by the same rules that the federal government is. Because your tax payers dollars are a large part of the funding that is given out by the government, income restrictions is the name of the game. How would you feel if James Doe was able to use your money to send his daughter, Jane Doe to college, although his salary was five times the amount as yours? I wouldn't like it, and I don't think you would either. If that were the case, many rich families would simply apply for grants, and save part or most of their money from their children's tuitions. I am not saying that all rich people would, but some families would apply with large financial assets.

Fellowships are for graduate students, and also cover a wide variety of topics in order to be eligible. When one of the commercials stated that you could get free money to write a book, I rushed out and bought the book, only to find out that the majority of the foundations listed that gave to my state were full of restrictions. Also, quite a few of the fellowships required that you live abroad for at least a minimal amount of time. How many working people can afford to travel abroad to write a book?

I am not taking away from any of the books or other forms of videos and media on free money. Once you understand the big picture, those type of books that give you a listing of grants, scholarships, and fellowships available to your state can be very helpful, and used as a resource repeatedly. I have bought one of the books three times. Every time I buy Mathew Lesko's book 3 times titled, Free Money, I ended up loaning it to a friend or co-worker to share the information listed in the book, and they never returned. It is worth repurchasing. It's like having a good health book that you refer to through the years, when you need to research a particular area. Can you practice as a doctor or nurse legally by owning the health book? No. If you own the reference book listing grants, you still have to understand WHAT a grant is, what rules apply to getting one, and what to do once you get it.

Scholarships cover a wide range of giving. My block club formed a nonprofit in order to give away scholarships to students that were graduating from high school, had good grades, and were considering college. The block club gave away $500 to the student chosen at the high school in the area.

Further, I read the guidelines where I was looking at a scholarship that you could access only if you were a Native American by birth. There are all kinds of guidelines, pre-requisites, and requirements that govern who get the scholarship or grant. An applicant has to understand the process.

My block club asked for an essay, with the topic changing annually. The essay had a deadline for the essay contest and then a date to announce the winner, and last, the date and place of the award ceremony. You might say that this was a lot in order to give away $500 a year. That is why it is usually important to ask the funder how much money is being given away with each round? Or if you do not want to be that direct, ask them for a copy of their annual report, which will give you the same information, and usually covers the last four years of funding.

There was a period when convicted felons could not apply for grants for college. In some states, that has been remedied. In the state of Ohio, if you have a drug trafficking charge or any of the other charges that are listed to deem you ineligible, you can now complete an approved drug treatment program, get a certificate, and become eligible. Remember to check with the financial aid office of the college you would like to attend to see what you can do to bypass the law. There are now ways around it for most state residents.

DIFFERENCES BETWEEN PROFIT AND NONPROFIT CORPS

There is an accountability with nonprofits that is not a necessity in profit corporations. For example, if you own a construction company, and you charge the client $90,000 to expand their home, and then you do not complete the job, the customer can do little, other than take you to civil court to attempt to recover their money back. In the nonprofit sector, complaints are investigated. The reason for this is because nonprofits are public and community organizations and receive some type of government funding, which means tax payers money. A nonprofit organization can be audited at any time, by funders and the IRS, and must keep public records.

Nonprofit organizations are labor-intensive, in that there is always sign-in sheets, monthly and annual program and financial reports, and constant streams of paperwork to complete. However, an agency that is doing a good job is eager to show off the numbers served, in order to continue to be at the top of the funders list. Attempt to put yourself in the shoes of the funder. Would you continue to fund an agency that has not shown any proof of how and where your funding dollars are spent? If an agency takes the initiative to go that extra mile and provide documentation, that agency will appear and remain at the top of funders list when it comes time to pass out awards. Awards equal dollars.

Below I have listed a profit and nonprofit budget, so that you can understand clearly the difference, which is usually displayed in the bottom line; what is left at the end of the year.

First let's start with an example of a profit budget from a family owned towing and snow removal company located in Ohio. After totaling receipts at the end of the year John Smith earned in $400,000 for 2005. His three employees were his son John Smith Jr., and his two nephews, Curtis Smith and Marlon Allen. He paid both his nephews $10,000 a year for part time, seasonal work, himself $50,000 a year, and his son $30,000 a year.

Smith's Towing, Inc.

Salaries	$100,000
Consultants	6,000
Equipment	2,000
Expenses	2,000
Admin/Overhead	10,000
120,000	total expenses
280,000	profit/balances

With a profit business, John can keep the profit and buy himself that new car, or whatever he chooses to do with it. John does not have to answer to anyone, or report anything, except tax authorities. Once his taxes are paid, the profit is his to do as he sees fit.

The Smith Community Center is a nonprofit corporation. For the first year, the agency also received $400,000, but instead of providing a towing service, the community center provided after school services to youth in the community. The money was received by the director and board, in the form of 3 grants. One from the county in the amount of $150,000, a second one from a community foundation in the amount of $150,000, and the other $100,000 from a private foundation. YOU DO NOT HAVE TO PAY GRANTS BACK. Many people confuse grants with loans. You have to be accountable with grant money. You are receiving tax payers and foundation dollars, in order to provide a service to the community.

Smith Community Center

Starting with $400,000 in grants

Salaries	$100,000
Consultants/contractors	$250,000
Equipment/supplies	39,000
Expenses	600
Admin/overhead	10,000
400	– balance

With a nonprofit organizational budget, the part-time workers are listed under the consultant or contractor line. Also supplies are always a need in the budget. An example of supplies would be books, paper, discs, and software for a community after school program. Equipment covers computers, copiers, and printers.

With a nonprofit business, you are given grant money, and expected to spend it on your budget. If you have anything left over at the end of the year, it should be minimal. That is the main reason why it is called a nonprofit.

The Helpful Highlights section lists a nonprofit operating budget.

Chapter 2: Helpful Highlights

Sample Donor List

Foundations

The Barra Foundation, Inc

Birmingham Foundation

The Bush Foundation

The Dan Foundation

Deer Creek Foundation

Doris Duke Charitable Foundation

The Ford Foundation

The Freeman Foundation

Gates Family Foundation

The Hearst Foundation

The Robert Wood Johnson Foundation

The Kresge Foundation

The Rockefeller Foundation

The Wallace Foundation

Anonymous (20)

Public Charities

California Healthcare Foundation

McCormick Tribune Foundation

Messouri Foundation for Health

The Pew Charitable Trusts

Rockefeller Family Fund

Youth Foundation, Inc.

Fannie Mae Foundation Fund

Washington Area Women's Foundation

The Wolpert Fund

The Sherwick Fund

The True-Mart Fund

Chisholm Memorial Fund

Candelaria Fund

The Chris Tensen Fund

Gara Fund

Corporations

Alcoa Foundation

Altria Foudnation

American Express Foundation

Avon Foundation, Inc.

The Coca Cola Company

IBM Corporation

The Merck Company Foundation

J.P. Morgan Chase & Co.

Morgan Stanley

Motorola Foundation

Pfizer Inc.

State Farm Companies Foundation

The U.P.S. Foundation (UPS)

Wells Fargo Foundation

The Xerox Foundation

Individuals

The England Family

The Castle Family

The Ferguson Family

The Bechtel Family

The Moran Family

The Dreyfus Family

The Turpin Family

The Walker Family

The Green Family

The Cohen Family

The Krieble Delmas Family

The Greenwall Family

Samuel H. Kress Family

Andrea Young Family

The Zellerbach Family

Chapter 3

Free Money Quiz

Now that you know more about grant money and where it comes from, its time to ask yourself, "Is this the field for me?" Your career should be challenging and fulfilling. They created different careers for different people. This is your chance to test yourself and see where you rate as a nonprofit director or manager.

The following quiz is a straight forward measurement. There are no trick questions. Answer either yes or no. The lists of skills were compiled from looking at successful nonprofit directors, talking to a few, and reading many accounts of what is a must in the character of a nonprofit administrative or management staff.

Ready? Let's do it.

Quiz

1. Are you self motivated?   yes ☐   no ☐

2. Do you delegate well?   yes ☐   no ☐

3. Are you detail oriented?   yes ☐   no ☐

4. Do you think outside the box?   yes ☐   no ☐

5. Do you work well under pressure?   yes ☐   no ☐

6. Are you outcome oriented?   yes ☐   no ☐

7. Do you network well?   yes ☐   no ☐

8. Do you adapt to change well?   yes ☐   no ☐

9. Are you a good record keeper?   yes ☐   no ☐

10. Do you dislike structured hours? yes ☐   no ☐

Total up how many yes answers you marked. Then look at next page for results.

If you scored 10-8 yes answers, you have the skills it takes to be a success in the nonprofit sector.

If you scored 7-5 yes answers, you need improvement. With completion of a few classes, you may be able to do well as a nonprofit management staff.

If you scored 4 and under, nonprofit management may not be the field for you. Research your options, and if still interested, volunteer at a local nonprofit organization. Agencies are always seeking for dedicated volunteers, as well as paid and un-paid internships.

Let's talk about why each skill is important in achieving success in the nonprofit profession.

Self-Motivation

This is one of the most important traits needed. Because nonprofits are funded by grants, you have to be a go getter. You have to multi-task. You have to follow the money.

Following the money one month may mean attending a Request for Proposal meeting in Washington D.C., in order to obtain a six-digit grant from Department of Housing and

Urban Development for emergency shelter for the home-less. The following month it could mean attending a RFP meeting with the county commissioners one day, United Way the next, and then meeting with a group of potential funders to offer a presentation on your agency services. There is no boss looking over your shoulder. Directors do not punch time cards. If you're not doing the job it will show in your bottom line-your funding coming in.

The mission that you are attempting to achieve has to be your motivator. You have to believe in what you are doing, and have the will to do it. If you do, the money will come, and help to motivate you further. There is no ceiling on how many grants a nonprofit can have, or how much money they are allowed to have. You truly reap what you sow in the nonprofit profession. The accountability comes with your board. Your board of trustees can fire you for under-performing. That occurs more in larger nonprofits that are already well-established. The success of the agency is measured on the amount of dollars a director brings in.

Delegates well

Imagine this. It's Thursday morning, and you walk into your office to begin your day. You have 20 phone calls to return, an irate parent holding on line one, two program reports due, and an RFP meeting at 10:00 am, in an hour. Time to delegate, do it accurately, and quick.

A good director is hands on, but you are only one person. Passing on some of your work load frees you to concentrate on bringing in the dollars.

Good management is also knowing who to delegate to. If one of your employees is not good at note taking, asking questions, or the entire grant process, you do not send that employee to do the job. Putting it in the hands of an incompetent person is as bad as not completing the task at all. The statement 'if you want something done right, do it yourself,' can not apply to all the multi-faceted tasks of running a nonprofit. Burn-out from the job is extremely common for nonprofit directors.

A good office manager along with a good program manager should be able to free you to attend RFP meetings, where you will run into other directors. The meetings are a good place to network and exchange stories about your program, as well as receive tips on upcoming RFP meetings that you may have missed. If your staff is not able to complete the tasks at hand, replace them. If you do not, you will burn out quickly.

Detail oriented

There are visionaries, and then there are people that carry out the vision. A nonprofit director has to be both. They have to be able to create or conceive the vision. Then set down and map out goals on how to make it happen.

Many people are visionaries. I have friends that tell me regularly, "I'd like to start a youth program," or "I'd like to start a half-way house." They have a good clear vision, but not a clue on how to do it, and no desire to put forth the effort to accomplish the tedious details of getting started. It is that detail oriented person that gets to work to complete their vision.

There are directors and managers that have a vision, sit back, and pay people to put it into place. That is a profit corporation. You can not be successful in running a nonprofit unless you understand the intricacies of the agency. You have to provide details of your programs for grants and reports. You are constantly detailing what your agency does in the course of the day.

You cannot fool funders with fluff. Funders like to talk to the director who ultimately will receive their check. It is considered an insult if the director is not available to speak with a funder and answer any questions they might have. It may be something simple like, "when you send forty children to the horse farm, how many staff to you send along with them?" That is a fair question. There are laws governing the ratio of adults to children that varies according to children's age range. A good director will be aware of that, and easily put the funder at ease about the agency's knowledge base. Know your program, and all the details about how it works.

Thinks outside the box

There are many nonprofits in the United States. In your area there is someone, somewhere with a similar program. Funders receive anywhere from one hundred proposals to 3000 proposals per quarter, vying for their dollars. There is mass competition in the funding cycle. All agencies want a piece of the monetary pie. Unfortunately, there is only one pie. How do you win? That's the question.

For years, agencies received the money year after year, without having to show outcomes of how their program benefited its targeted population. Most children's programs and summer camps were little more than babysitters, offering limited activities. Then the 90's brought what is called outcome measures. United Way offers training and certificates in this skill. The outcome is what you said you would do in the grant. How you measure it and provide proof is by developing or adopting tools. A good tool I use is an entrance survey, and an exit survey that I design according to the program.

If an agency is providing housing, then you provide housing with a training component. If a summer camp has field trips, you provide horse camps or even golfing lessons. Your aim should be to strive to be different and better, not the same as other agencies.

Thinking inside the box means to conform to traditional thinking and planning. In order to be successful in obtaining the money in today's funding arena, you have to ask yourself, how can you provide quality programming to the community without being repetitious? Be innovative. Be creative. Think outside of tradition in the area you are attempting to provide service delivery.

Works well under pressure

A nonprofit director is under constant pressure. An RFP meeting may offer an application and grant dollars on March 1, due March 20th. Most directors will have more than one grant coming in at a time, and be working on more than one component of their program at a time. The exception is if you are looking to provide a simple service, like dinner for the homeless. That's one service, one outcome, and probably no more than one grant, with the full use of volunteers to compensate the chores not covered in the grant.

The juggling act is needed if you have an agency that is managing or attempting to build a full staffed, multi-faceted program agency. An example would be an agency that offers computer training, literary, GED, and job readiness training. All four services require accessing a different pot of money. Many times, all four grants will be due within the same period. I've had to work around the clock for three days in order to get my grants in on time. After completion, I'm then racing to the funder the morning of the deadline to hand deliver the requested 6 copies, or to a post office to mail priority mail. Also, Murphy's Law does come into play. My copier seems to shut down under pressure. That's why it's important to also keep two contingency copiers at your fingertips. Mines was a 24-hour Kinko's located in downtown Cleveland on East 9th, and a 24-hour Copy Max, located on Mayfield near the freeway exit. Pressure is part of the job for a nonprofit director.

Outcome oriented

I talked a little bit about outcome measures as one of the skills needed for success.

In a grant to the county commissioners for an after-school program, we stated that "25% of our students would improve at least one letter grade during the upcoming school year." That is a clear, concise outcome. So how did we prove it? By creating an entrance survey listing the student's incoming letter grades, with a zerox copy of their first report cards attached to the survey. Then we designed our program curriculum to focus on improving each student's academic grade. We offered tutors that worked with each student for a minimum of 30 minutes each day after school. At the end of the school year, we simply attached the final report card to our exit survey on each student. That's a clear measurement tool, displaying clear outcomes. Nothing fancy needed but a copy of the student's report cards.

It was a time when providing the same service for years was enough to get funding from a variety of sources. Today funders are willing to take a chance on a new agency that is providing outcomes.

Funders do except that your agency may not always meet the goals listed. Say that to them. List your obstacles in your next application or program report, as well as what you've put in place to correct the problem. The first time we only improved 15% of students, due to a large turnover of foster care students. Our second year we improved 45%, which was well over the stated goal, by enrolling a more diverse kind of student, while still also helping foster care children.

Showing real outcomes to funders will get you the money and keep it coming in.

Networks well

The quickest way to build visibility for your agency is to partnership. Learn how many schools are in your area. Also churches, hospitals, and other businesses. Let the community know you're there, and the services you are providing.

If the neighborhoods have a block watch or block club, attend the meetings. Invite the community in. It is no such thing as over-networking. You can never do enough.

At every public event, make your agency a part of the structure by giving door prizes as simple as ink pens with your agency's name on them. The cost of this type of advertisement is minimal. It is important to network with banks in your area. Banks sponsor events in order to support a good cause and attract customers.

It is no such thing as operating a successful nonprofit alone. One of the easiest ways to become visible in your area is to establish a neighborhood clean up day with student teams, and have one of the businesses partner by offering refreshments to your volunteers.

Attend school events to network with teachers and other staff. Be a guest at a neighborhood church board of directors meeting to see how you can assist them in furthering their mission.

Obtain a list of businesses from your Chamber of Commerce and get to know your neighbors and surroundings, and also your competitors in service delivery. They may not welcome you with open arms, but take the time to visit other agencies that provide similar services as yours.

Some initiatives will fund a partnership or collaboration of agencies, businesses and churches before they will fund a single agency. It's a larger service horizon for their bucks.

Never stop networking, even when you're considered off the clock.

Adapts to change well

The world is constantly changing around us. What is sufficient in today's work force, may become obsolete in the near future. The biggest change and challenge for agencies over the last decade is technology advances.

Computers, e-mail, teleconferencing, Power Point, and many more technological advances have made the jobs of staff nationwide more efficiently. Today it is just as common for a person to exchange e-mails, as it used to be phone numbers. This change encouraged technological upgrading for a large number of agencies. Discount rates are offered for new computers and software has been offered for nonprofits by filling out a simple application.

However, there are a few agencies that refuse to go digital. "If it is not broke, do not fix it." Is what the creatures of habit have rallied. With the test of time, and other agencies becoming further advanced in technology, the agency funding stream will eventually dry up. As agency leaders, we have to be able to change with the times.

A current change is the requirement that an agency be bilingual in Spanish and English in order to receive federal funding by the year 2010. Are directors on top of this by offering Spanish language initiatives to their employees? They should be. These type of changes occur regularly in the nonprofit sector.

Also, with each President comes a new initiative. That means the dollars are directed in the area that the President requests. An associate of mine told me that he left the nonprofit sector to open his own construction business. He said the reason was because he kept having to change or tweak his services in order to accommodate the funders and remain in the circle of funded agencies. After 17 years, he gave his career as director up.

There are constant changes required of an agency in order to remain fully funded. You have to keep up with potential changes by reading the trade magazines for nonprofits, and be willing to constantly change, evolve, and grow.

Good Record Keeper

Out of the ten skills needed to be a successful director, this is one where I fall short. Because I know that this is not my strong point, it was important that I hired a staff person that was strong in record keeping and documentation.

All money spent has to be accounted for and documented. Nonprofits are funded by tax payers dollars, or foundation dollars. Funders want to know where their money is going. Gas purchasing on the way to RFP meetings has to be documented, and the receipt recorded as well as purchases. I always told myself that I would record things like gasoline, mileage, or a printer ribbon for my office printer later. Later never came, therefore it was charged out of my pocket and salary because I did not have a receipt to attach to my monthly financial statement.

You have to keep a good record of all money coming in and out of the agency. You also have to keep clear documentation of program delivery, such as program sign-in sheets. Most funders require some type of program report. Your program report will display the number of people served, and other interval information about your agency.

Once your agency budget grows, it is smart to invest in good business software such as QuickBooks, Peachtree accounting software, or Microsoft money. These types of software allows you to make simple entries daily, weekly, and monthly, and then manipulate the date entered into clear detailed graphs, charts, and spreadsheets in a matter of minutes.

Nonprofit records have to be available for the public for a period of up to four years. Also you can be audited during the four year period of any funding cycle. Keep good, clear easy-to-read records of finances and programs.

<u>Dislike structured hours</u>

This is listed last, but just as important as all of the rest of the skills and traits needed. Some people hate change, are creatures of habit, love structure and for everything to be done at a certain time, on time. If that is you, then it is going to be hard to adjust to your required role in the nonprofit world. During the end of the month, when program reports are due, your hours are never ending. If you're lucky, you'll work less hours the beginning of the month. Also you cannot count on being off every weekend. Some days may start at eight a.m. Others may start at seven, or even ten o'clock a.m. Your hours will fluctuate from day-to-day, unless you are a small agency, with a very small budget.

Why can't you get off work at five o'clock every day like your corporate counterparts? It's because grants and program reports is how you are paid. If they are not done by the agreed, set deadlines, your funder that pays your salary will simply hold your check until they are completed. Profit businesses benefit by whatever product or service they are selling. There is usually no deadline. If a profit executive decides to go home and end sales, it is done. No losses. Nonprofits rely on grants for funding and to meet payroll. That's how it works.

Traditional fundraisers include car washes, dinners, and family field trips. These events occur on the weekend. It is a part of your job description to be visibly present during these events.

During the week you may be able to structure hours to work at home instead of in the office. I often wrote proposals in the morning from home, putting in the second half of the day in the office. Every work week held a new and different challenge. No two months were the same.

If you enjoy moving around, setting new goals and challenges, and constantly multi-tasking, then the nonprofit field may be the best field for you. Every day, every month, each year holds new challenges.

The Free Money Quiz was designed to assist you in evaluating your strong and weak points. Many of these traits apply to profit businesses as well. You will find out that in the big picture, there is not a large difference in running a nonprofit, versus a profit corporation.

If the Quiz has peaked your interest, the next chapter will prepare you on How to get some of the billions of dollars available to you from funders and donors. Look at these chapters as your "No Money Down" plan to success.

Chapter 4

How do I get the money?

There is only one way to capitalize on the funding stream of money in abundance. Start a nonprofit agency or organization. A nonprofit gets the real money. You are probably wondering as you sit on the couch watching the news, 'how in the world do I do that?' If you have a passion about something that can also be identified as a community or urban problem, you can turn your passion into a nonprofit project.

There are four major steps to setting up a nonprofit:
1. Pick a name, check the availability through the secretary of state.
2. Set up a nonprofit corporation with the Secretary of State.
3. Obtain a tax identification number through IRS (Internal Revenue Service).
4. File the IRS Form 1023.

The Federal Secretary of State governs the entire country, and sets the basic standards for business structures. Each state has its own elected Secretary of State that has a few other duties. Included in those duties are making available business forms, having a name availability research phone line, and other business related services in order to assist you in keeping your business in good standing.

DECIDING THE NAME OF YOUR AGENCY

Picking a name is very important. When you decide on a name, you should already have a general idea of what service you would like to provide, and your target population.

What that means is that you can not properly pick a name until you have narrowed down what you want to do. For example, you attend a high school graduation of your neighbor. After the service, you network, and congratulate the students who received honor roll and perfect attendance awards. You ask the students if they are going to college or not. A few of them explain to you that although they plan to go, there is some upfront costs that they do not have, such as application fees, testing fees, and postage. They tell you that they plan to get a job immediately to cover all costs associated with the pre-college applications. You go home, and the conversation bother you so much that you decide to do something about it. You realize that you are not John D. Rockefeller, but you also know that you can decide to help a minimum of two students a year, by giving them $500 each to assist them with the pre-college registration fees.

You decide to take action. You ask your co-worker's father for free advice, who is an accountant. He tells you it is a very good idea. You start the process, and began to establish what your guidelines will be for accessing award dollars. If your name is Smith, you decide to call your nonprofit the Smith Scholarship Fund. The fund has the potential to grow into something major by the number of grants you receive, and the amount of money you raise under the rules of the nonprofit if you decide to keep it simple you can have one event a year to cover all costs of the award, and continue to keep your days and nights your own. This is an example of a local neighborhood project. This type of project is usually limited to a particular neighborhood or high school. Geographic location is listed in the guidelines as one of the limitations of the grant. You can give two scholarships away for the rest of your life, and pass the family nonprofit down to your children and grandchildren, without ever decreasing or increasing the cause. Also, for the record, it is an excellent tax write off. All costs pertaining to the nonprofit is a tax write-off. I am not an accountant. I do advise anyone that is interested in beginning a nonprofit to seek out an accountant that will offer good advice in this area without charging a fee. Look for one that offers a free consultation.

The nonprofit that I assisted in setting up to fuel my own passion was J.U.M.P. Inc. I started this nonprofit with my daughter Tee. Although we wished to service two different target age groups our passions joined together.

Tee wanted to help children between the ages of 6 to 16 with after-school programming and mentoring, because she loved kids. She was also having a challenge in finding after-school programs that were cost-effective, with a strong educational objective. She had my Granddaughter to consider to be able to say strongly what she didn't want. A standard babysitting program, where children came from school and drew pictures or watched T.V. was unacceptable to her. She wanted snacks served, homework time, exposure to cultures, and a play time that incorporated learning life skills. Her ideas were excellent, and caught on quick to funders. We learned quickly that funders were also tired of giving money to babysitters, but had no visible alternatives. Funders are people too, not machines. Some of the funders of that component of the agency were probably mothers or grandmothers.

My passion involved the older population. I was interested in ages 16 to 25 years of age. William Clinton, our President of the United States at the time, had recently passed the Welfare-To-Work Act that made it mandatory for every state to participate in national time limits. Women that had been on welfare for generations were forced to observe the time limits, and use the given time to get a job. From working with welfare recipients in the past, we knew that without comprehensive help, a lot of children were going to be hungry and in trouble. The Act insisted on moving women with no marketable skills, little education, no interviewing knowledge or any concept of time management into employable citizens. Larger Bureaucratic agencies did not have a clue of how to achieve this goal. We presented my proposal to funders, receiving plenty of funding supporters. We knew what had to be done. A lot of the population had to be taken by the hand literally, and worked on as a whole. Our program offered GED, job readiness mock interviews, job training and free daycare for program participants. We even offered a ride back and forth to the program by van for women with children and no transportation. We beat the larger agencies out because all of their clients were falling through the cracks. How could you expect a student to come to computer class five days a week, with literacy issues, and no one to watch her children? How would she get to the program, when transportation was not an allotment from welfare, or daycare, until a job was found? These were the type of barriers to success that we addressed and conquered. I want to clarify that some of the women were a lot easier than others. What I described were women with more than one barrier to employment. Some women knew how to fill out a job application, and had graduated from high school with some college. The latter population needed to strengthen their computer skills to become more marketable. That task took about six weeks, through on-hand computer training classes. We really had our hands full, but we loved every minute of it.

In deciding what type of service you want to offer, you should also consider the restrictions if you are a convicted felon, or plan to hire anyone on your staff that is a felon.

There are currently no restrictions on felons starting nonprofit organizations. In fact, a few of the best agencies by way of service delivery has been started by felons. Prior drug addicts create drug rehabilitation houses and centers. Runaway teenagers later grow up and start homes for runaway girls. Domestic Violence victims that survive start the most effective shelters and halfway houses for women recovering from domestic violence. A large number of people have a passion for projects that serve the underserved. I don't know the percentage, but in a lot of cases, the passion to change something comes from your own personal experience or either what you have witnessed in family, friends, or a loved one.

Currently, there are two standard restrictions on convicted felons in the nonprofit sector. There is a national house bill that restricts felons from working with children under 16, and also senior citizens 65 or older. In other words, ages zero to sixteen is restricted along with ages 65 and older for long term care. What does long term care mean? It means that if you are a convicted felon, check with your state to see what the guidelines are for the house bill, and the exceptions. States were allowed to create their own exceptions. For instance, in the state of New York, if your felony is more than seven years old, and you have remained out of trouble, the house bill does not apply, and you have no restrictions. Some states have even more lenient laws offering some reciprocity to the bill. Ohio has always been one of the most conservative states in the country. In Ohio it doesn't matter if your felony is twenty years old. You are forbidden from working directly with children or elderly. However, remember the words "long-term care". If you are a felon, they are very important words. Long term care also means direct service. When starting J.U.M.P. Inc. with my daughter, I was a convicted felon. In order to avoid being in any type of local., state, or federal violation, I called the licensing agencies for after school programs in the county of Cuyahoga, where our first site was located, as well as the state licensing agency in Columbus. I was instructed that I could not do direct day-to-day service, but that I could do all of the administrative duties, such as grants, program reports, taxes, etc. I was elated with that news. I had no intention or interest in being directly involved in the day to day care of 60 active children. That's 60 different personalities, and 60 little people all competing for attention of some sort. I left all aspects of the after-school programs to my daughter, who loved the drama and excitement of having 60 children in her presence each day. I was content doing the hiring, firing, and grant writing for the agency.

Between working with the welfare-to-work mothers and the job readiness workshop we offered for males ages 16 to 25, my plate was full. I also had no desire to work directly with the elderly. So remember, prior to choosing a name make sure that you haven't picked a project that has restrictions.

The second area where felons cannot participate is Bingo in Ohio. Bingo and other fundraising events are governed by the state attorney general, and varies from state to state. All states do not have this rule. A lot of people expect a Bingo component to their nonprofit, so make sure that you call your state Attorney general's office and have them mail you a copy of the rules in your state.

Now that you have decided what type of service you want to offer, its time to move your project forward to determine the name of your nonprofit. There are no mandatory names that you have to use for a nonprofit. If you are thinking about making your cause a part of a family legacy, consider using your last name as part of the title.

For example, my last name is Turpin. There could be a Turpin Community Center, Turpin Community Services Organization, Turpin Services, Inc. Turpin Entertainment, Inc, Turpin Theatre Ensemble, Turpin Credit Counseling, Turpin Scholarship Fund, or R.J. Turpin Foundation. Get the point?

You can also use acronyms which is what my daughter Tee and I did. Whatever name you decide, think it out well, because once you set up a nonprofit corporation you do not want to change the name. When marketing yourself to receive funding and donors, you will be asked to explain and defend your name and your agency services repeatedly. If you possess passion about your project, it will rub off on potential funders and donors. If you don't, that can also be detected. Having a lack of enthusiasm about your project can lead to your demise. Like a profit business, you have to be able to market yourself and your idea. 90% of the public do not want fluff. In this day and age, most people recognize crap because they have heard it many times. Know your cause.

After determining the name you would like for your agency to be called, the next step is to contact the Secretary of State. Each state has a secretary of state that are smaller units, primarily governed by the United States Secretary of State office. There are basic rules and laws that apply to the entire country.

However, each state is allowed to implement internal local laws that apply specifically to your state. These laws are mandated by the elected secretary of state officials. If you vote, he or she campaigned to be elected, and you should be familiar with these candidates. If you're not, add that to your list of things to do and learn to be the best agency. If you're not registered to vote, its time to.

Owning and running a business is much like entering a professional race. How can you have a chance of winning or scoring when you don't know how to reach the location of the race, don't know who is competing, and don't know the rules or players? Taking that extra step in business is what separates the winners from the losers. There are three ways to contact your secretary of state:

1. By U.S. mail
2. By telephone
3. By internet

I've set up many businesses as a consultant for people in profit and nonprofit sectors, therefore, I can say that all contact methods are equally effective. The only difference would be time and preference. I've had clients of all walks of life that do not like the internet. They prefer the verbal interaction of a live operator. Then there are people who like to take their time, review the forms, and mail them back at their leisure. U.S. mail works best for them.

Many people are now comfortable with the internet. If you email the Secretary of State staff, they will return your email promptly with the reply to your name availability search request.

The forms you need to name and set up your nonprofit corporation are available by accessing the website. Once you access the Secretary of State home page, click on Business Forms. Scroll down the list until you see the form you're seeking, and then click on it. Once the form is displayed, print out the blank form. It's that simple. The forms database will allow you to print out the form labeled Form 532-Initial Articles of Incorporation.

COMPLETING NONPROFIT ARTICLES

The filing fee for the name registration is $50.00. The filing fee for the Articles of Incorporation form is $125.00. The current fee will be listed on the form and subject to change, so make sure that the amount you send in is verified, so that it doesn't delay the setting up of your business.

The first part of the form reads: (1)
Check only one Box

1.☐ Articles of Incorporation 2.☐ Articles of Incorporation 3.☐ Articles of Incorporation Profit   Nonprofit   Professional   Profession _____

For setting up a nonprofit, you check box 2. Remember, before you complete this form, you should have already checked the availability of the name you've chosen with the secretary of state. There are no short cuts. Using the name of a business that is registered to someone else is illegal in all states, and will get you shut down, and fined large sums of money and sometimes prosecuted.

The section part of form 532 states: (2)

<u>Sample</u>

First: Name of Corporation <u>ABC Community Center Inc.</u> **Second:** Location   <u>Cleveland</u>   <u>Cuyahoga</u>   (City)   (County) **Effective Date (Optional):** Date specified can be no more than 90 days after the date of _____ filing. If a date is specified the date must be on or after the _____ date of filing. ☐ Check here if additional Provisions are attached

This section is self-explanatory. My suggestion is to keep your filing simple. If you're not sure of start dates or provisions, it is not necessary to fill out these lines. Pay attention. Putting the state on the form instead of the county is a common mistake and will delay your filing.

The next section of the application states: (3) Complete the information in this section only if box (2) or (3) is checked

---

Third: Purpose Corporation is formed

To provide recreational services to at-risk youth and their families, who are disadvantaged. Services include after school programs, summer camp, and seasonal field trips.

Sample

Section 3 is very important in setting up your nonprofit. You will use this information repeatedly each time you apply for a grant. You will also use it on the I.R.S. 1023 application to become a tax exempt organization.

Funders will request a copy or view your filing before extending funding, so give this area a lot of thought. Your services should coincide with your mission statement. What you list in section 3 will be public information.

The fourth part of this form reads: (4)
Complete the information in this section of (1) or (3) is checked

---

Fourth: The number of shares which the corporation is authorized to have outstanding (Please state if shares are common or preferred and list par value if any)

_____   _____   _____

(no of shares)   (type)   per value

Sample

Nonprofit applicants do <u>NOT</u> fill out this section, so we will move on.

The fifth part of the form reads: (5)

Fifth: The following is the names and addresses of the individuals who are to serve as initial Directors

---

(Name)

(Street)

(City)   (State)   (Zip Code)

(Name)

(Street)

(City)	(State)	(Zip Code)

(Name)

(Street)

(City)	(State)	(Zip code)

Note: P.O. Box Addresses are NOT acceptable

A nonprofit organization has to have a board of directors. A board of directors and a board of Trustees mean exactly the same thing, as the word attorney and lawyer. The board member governs the affairs of a nonprofit corporation. If there are any misuses of funds, the board of directors are legally responsible. It is not important to enlist people as your permanent board. The names listed on this form are your temporary board, until your first board meeting. Meeting time, places, and schedule is decided and detailed in your agency bylaws.

The process of finding board members should be thought out for your permanent board. For your temporary board, as long as you have the person's full permission it's fine. You can use any or all of the temporary board members listed as your permanent board. They must agree to sign the federal I.R.S. 1023 form, and be voted in at the first official board meeting to become permanent board members.

The next part of the filing is mandatory. You cannot form a nonprofit or profit corporation without a statutory agent.

<u>Sample</u>

Complete the information in this section if box (2) or (3) is checked

Original Appointment of Statutory Agent

The undersigned being appointed by

A majority of the incorporators of ABC Community Center Inc.

hereby appoint named to be statutory agent upon whom any process, notice or demand required or permitted by stature to be served on the corporation may be served. The compete address of the agent is

_____

(Name)

_____

(Street) P.O. Box not acceptable

_____

(City)

Must be authentic and authorized

representative   _____   _____

                  Authorized Representative   Date

                  _____   _____

                  Authorized Representative   Date

Acceptance of Appointment

The undersigned _____named herein as the statutory agent for ABC Community Center, Inc

Signature _____

(Statutory Agent)

To put it in simple terms, your statutory agent is your public contact for the business. Credit card applications, notice of filing expirations, and public inquiries are mailed to your agent. It is very important to keep your agent contact information current and updated. You can do this free of charge by simply mailing in a change of address form, signed by your agent. The agent does not have to have direct involvement in the day-to-day operation of the business. Also the agent is not legally responsible for the business. The board of directors are. An agents responsibilities are similar to a public relations contact for your agency.

There is no minimum or maximum time limit that your agent receives notices for the business. A statutory agent can remain the same for the duration of the business, or the name can change as often as you like. Just remember to complete the proper secretary of state forms including a change of address or change of statutory agent.

The last part of your state filing is the required signatures of the incorporators of the business.

The form reads as follows:
Required
Must be authentic (signed)
By an authorized representative

_____   _____
   Authorized Representative   Date

_____
   Print Name_____

_____

_____

   Print Name_____

_____

_____

   Print Name_____

_____

There is space for no more than 3 incorporators. When mailing the form, you can expedite service. The cost is an additional $100 added to the filing fee. There is a different address listed on the top of the form for express service. The normal turn around time to receive your certificate and charter number is 2 to 3 weeks. A personal or business check takes longer because they wait on it to clear. A bank or post office money order is the best form of payment.

That completes the second step of setting up a nonprofit corporation.

THE EIN FORM

The third step is setting up a nonprofit, 501-C- 3 agency is to fill out an Employer Identification number request form. The proper term for the form is an SS-4 form.

This is a tax identification number. When you apply for your EIN, you will automatically start to receive tax filing information, in conjunction with the business structure you listed on your form.

You cannot complete this process until you have received the certificate listing the business charter number from the secretary of state filing.

The reason why is because one of the questions asks for the charter number of your corporation. Also we recommend that you have the completed form in front of you if you apply for an EIN by telephone.

There are 3 ways to apply for an EIN:
By U.S. Mail
By telephone
By internet

By telephone, you are issued a temporary EIN number immediately, once you give the staff person the information off the form. The reason why you need the form is because they ask you questions according to the box number of the forms. For example, box one would be the legal name of the business. Your permanent EIN takes approximately 2 to 3 weeks to arrive in the mail.

THE 1023 APPLICATION

The last part to setting up a nonprofit corporation is completing the IRS 1023 Application for Exemption, and then mailing it into IRS with the required processing fee. The only way you won't need the mail in fee is if you don't plan on making any money or receiving grants for the first couple of years. People will try to cut corners by not sending in the full amount. If you're setting up an agency with the intention of offering services, send the IRS the full fee. It is a one time set up payment.

The application is detailed and labor intensive. I am not going to attempt to break down the application. I am not an accountant or attorney. Knowledge in both areas is along with experience in completing the application.

There is a checklist at the beginning of the application to help you prepare your filing. A few of the things listed on your checklist is:

1. Your certificate from the Secretary of State, listing your charter number.

2. Your notification letter from IRS with your assigned EIN on it.

3. A list of board members, with full addresses included.

4. Percentage of each activity your agency will be attempting to conduct.
5. At least 2 years prior financial statements OR 2 to 3 years of projected income
6. A copy of your agency by laws that will be used to govern agency policy.

The following pages gives you a glimpse of what your by laws should consist of.

ABC Community Center will be governed at all times by no less than 5 board of trustees, with three of the trustees being officers. The Officers to be held are President, Vice President, Treasurer, and Secretary, with the President and Vice President actually as a combined role during the first year of service.

The maximum number of board members can be any odd number. A meeting can be held by conference call, email, or in person. Meetings will be held on the last Thursday of the month. The secretary will be responsible for taking, recording and transcribing the meetings, and making sure all board members receive a copy of the record. An emergency meeting can be called within 24 hours notice by a minimum of 3 board members. The president will decide the place and time for regular board meetings as well as emergency meetings.

Election of Officers

The president is a life long assignment. He can transfer all responsibility and power to a designee of his choice.

All other board officers will be nominated and elected on record and if no designee is named the board will elect a presiding president. All other board officers will serve a 3 year term as officers, but can remain a member of the board of trustees by votes to be held annually, for renewable terms, with no term limit. The meetings and procedures will be conducted according to Roberts Rules of order.

<u>Board Officers Duties</u>

The President facilitates the meetings, and calls to order as well as propose to adjourn the meeting, and authorized signer of checks.

Also responsible for signing all grants and 990's for the agency. The Vice President acts as president in the absence of the president during meetings. Also handles all staff complaints and customer issues by using conflict resolution techniques.

The treasurer will give monthly reports of agency progress, and be an authorized person on the bank account of the agency, and also look into ways to make the money work for the agency. He/she will bring ideas to the board to be voted on. This position cannot be held by a felon.

The Secretary will provide a copy of the board agenda, stating new business and any other matters to be discussed. He/She will keep and store accurate minutes of the meetings for no less than four years, as required by IRS standards. If a Sergeant of Arms is elected, they will keep order during the meeting, and follow proper compliance according to Roberts Rules of Order.

Agency Finances

All monies will go to the treasurer for deposit, after being signed and accounted for by the President. Only the president's signature is needed for any amount of checks. The treasurer can sign a check for up to $1000, with full signature authority. Any check exceeding the Treasurers signature limit has to be double endorsed by the president.

The Executive Director also has a $1000 signature limit, except for payroll checks. The E.D. has a payroll limit of $2500. The exception is when the E.D. and the President is the same individual.

Board Payment

The board of trustees is a voluntary position, along with the officers. However, a quarterly stipend of no more than $200 may be applied for in writing to the board president. If a member is on a special fund campaign or project, to assist with costs such as postage, paper, and travel, the stipend applies.

Get the drift?

Some other headings that may go in the context of your bylaws are:

- Board Retreats
- Board Hiring
- Donations

Last, there are a few things that are mandatory as part of your agency bylaws. They are:

Agency Restrictions

The agency cannot campaign for or against candidates for public office, and political lobbying is restricted.

If an agency makes a profit from activities unrelated to its nonprofit purpose, it must pay taxes on the profit, but up to $1000 or unrelated income can be earned tax-free.

Upon Dissolution of Agency

The assets of the agency must be irrevocably dedicated to charitable, educational, religious, or similar purposes. If the nonprofit dissolves, any assets it owns must be transferred to another 501 (C) (3) organization. The organization that is to receive assets upon dissolution of the agency does not have to be named. All assets will be dedicated to an active 501 (C) (3) agency located in the state of _____.

Amendments of Bylaws

Other than listed throughout the bylaws, the organization will follow general procedure of the Roberts Rules of Order to govern the organization and its meetings.

All amendments to the Bylaws or the agency mission and type of services are to be made in submitting to the Secretary of State, including any fees, and to the IRS for matter of record.

The Helpful Highlights section contains a few forms for those that are visual in understanding how the process works.

Helpful Highlights

The first part of this section gives you a look at the sample Initial Articles of Incorporation, used throughout the United States. The U.S. Secretary of State sets the standard and the prices. Your state office offers the form with contact information for each state. The sample forms are from the State of Ohio Secretary of State.

Chapter Four   1. <u>Helpful Highlights</u>

Instructions for Initial Articles of Incorporation

I. Select a name for your corporation.

A. The name you choose for your corporation MUST BE AVAILABLE FOR REGISTRATION. (ORC 1701.05)

To be considered available for registration, your proposed name must be distinguishable upon the records of the secretary of state from prior registrations of corporations, trade names, limited liability companies, limited liability partnership.

A name is not considered distinguishable from another name if it only differs in one or more of the following ways:

1. The use of the word corporation, company, incorporated, limited or any abbreviation of those words.

2. The use of any articles, conjunctions, contraction, abbreviation, or punctuation.

3. The use of a different tense or number of the same word.

4. Phonetic spellings. (i.e., Quick v. Kwik)

5. Use of prepositions. (i.e., Galaxy of Homes v. Galaxy Homes)

6. Use of the same letter or initial. (i.e., A. Cable v. AA Cable)

7. Use of possessive. (i.e., Doyle Motors v. Doyles Motors)

PLEASE NOTE THAT THIS LIST IS NOT ALL INCLUSIVE

AVAILABILITY OF A NAME MAY BE CHECKED BY CALLING 1-877-SOS-FILE, OR TO ASSURE YOUR PROPOSED TITLE WILL BE AVAILABLE FOR REGISTRATION, YOU MAY FILE A NAME RESERVATION PRIOR TO INCORPORATING.

Your proposed name will not be available for registration if it indicates or implies that it is connected with a government agency of the state of Ohio, another state or the United States.

The name of the corporation must end with or include "Company", "Co.", "Corporation", "Corp.", "Incorporated", or "Inc."

PLEASE NOTE: INCORPORATION UNDER A PARTICULAR NAME IS NOT AUTHORIZATION FROM THE SECRETARY OF STATE TO USE A PARTICULAR NAME. INCORPORATION UNDER A PARTICULAR NAME MEANS THAT THE NAME IS AVAILABLE FOR REGISTRATION PURSUANT TO THE NAME AVAILABILITY STANDARD LISTED ABOVE.

II. The articles of incorporation must indicate the city, village or township AND county in which the corporation is to be located. (ORC 1701.04, 1702.04)

Note: Entering the effective date is optional. If the date field is left blank, the effective date will be the date the filing is received. If a date is entered, it can <u>not</u> be more than 90 days <u>after</u> the date of receipt.

III. The articles must set forth the purpose for which the corporation is formed. (ORC 1701.04) (OPTIONAL IF BOX (1) IS CHECKED)

A. A corporation may be formed under this chapter for any purpose or combination of purposes for which individuals lawfully may associate themselves, except that, if the Revised Code contains special provisions pertaining to the formation of any designated type of corporation other than a professional association, as defined in section 1785.01 of the ORC, a corporation of that type shall be formed in accordance with the special provisions.

Chapter Four   <u>Helpful Highlights</u>

B. A corporation formed under Chapter 1702 of the ORC must contain a specific purpose for which the corporation is formed.

IV. The articles must indicate the number of shares of stock which the corporation is authorized to issue, together with the express terms, if any, of the shares. (ORC 1701.04(A)(4)). If no express terms stated shares, will be listed as no par value.

V. The articles must be accompanied by an original appointment of agent. (ORC 1701.04(D))

VI. The address listed for the statutory agent must contain a street and number. Post office box addresses and "building" addresses i.e., 100 Big Tower are not acceptable.

VII. The named statutory agent must acknowledge and accept the appointment of agent. (ORC 1701.07(B))

VIII. The filing fee for articles of incorporation is based upon the number of shares authorized in your articles. If you have authorized 1,500 shares or less in your articles of incorporation, your filing fee will be $125.00. If you wish to authorize more than 1,500 shares, your filing fee can be calculated by the standards set fourth in (ORC 111.16(A)92)). If you need assistance in calculating your filing fee, you may contact 1-877-SOS-FILE

VIIII. All of the incorporators must sign the articles of incorporation, and a majority of the same incorporators must sign the original appointment of statutory agent. (ORC 1701.04 and 1701.07)

PLEASE NOTE: A "SUBCHAPTER S" STATUS IS A TAX DESIGNATION. A "SUBCHAPTER S" STATUS MUST BE SECURED FROM THE INTERNAL REVENUE SERVICE. IN ADDITION, NOTICE OF A "SUBCHAPTER S" ELECTION MUST BE PROVIDED TO THE OHIO DEPARTMENT OF TAXATION (ORC 5733.09 (B)). FOR INFORMATION CONCERNING QUALIFICATIONS OR REQUIREMENTS FOR "SUBCHAPTER S" STATUS, YOU WILL NEED TO CONTACT THE IRS.

ORIGINAL APPOINTMENT OF STATUTORY AGENT

I. Profit and non-profit articles of incorporation must be accompanied by an original appointment of agent. ORC 1701.07(B), 1702.06(B)

II. The statutory agent for a corporation may be : (a) a natural person who is a resident of Ohio, or (b) an Ohio corporation or a foreign profit corporation licensed in Ohio, which has a business address in this state and is explicitly authorized by its articles of incorporation to act as a statutory agent. ORC 1701.07(A), 1702.06(A)

III. An original appointment of agent form must be signed by at least a majority of the incorporators of the corporation 1701.07 (B), 1702.06(B). These signatures must be the same as the signatures on the articles of incorporation.

Chapter Four   2. Helpful Highlights

Prescribed by:

Ohio Secretary of State
Central Ohio: (614) 466-3910
Toll Free: 1-877-SOS-FILE (1-877-767-3453)

www.sos.state.oh.us
e-mail: busserv@sos.state.oh.us

Expedite this Form: (Select One)

Mail Form to one of the Following:

○ Yes   PO Box 1390
         Columbus, OH 43216
*** Requires an additional fee of $100 ***

○ No   PO Box 670
         Columbus, OH 43216

INITIAL ARTICLES OF INCORPORATION
(For Domestic Profit or Nonprofit)
Filing Fee $125.00

THE UNDERSIGNED HEREBY STATES THE FOLLOWING:

(CHECK ONLY ONE (1) BOX)

(1) ☐ Articles of Incorporation Profit	(2) ☐ Articles of Incorporation Nonprofit	(3) ☐ Articles of Incorporation Professional (170-ARP)
(113-ARF) ORC 1701	(114-ARN) ORC 1702	Profession _____ ORC 1785

Complete the general information in this section for the box checked above.

FIRST: Name of Corporation   _____

SECOND: Location   _____   _____
                        (City)   (County)

Effective Date (Optional)   _____   Date specified can be no more than 90 days after date of filing. If a date is specified,
                              (mm/dd/yyyy)   the date must be a date on or after the date of filing.

☐ Check here if additional provisions are attached

Complete the information in this section if box (2) or (3) is checked. Completing this section is optional if box (1) is checked.

THIRD: Purpose for which corporation is formed

_____

_____

_____

_____

Complete the information in this section if box (1) or (3) is checked.

FOURTH: The number of shares which the corporation is authorized to have outstanding (Please state if shares are common or preferred and their par value if any)

_____   _____   _____
(No. of Shares)   (Type)   (Par Value)

(Refer to instructions if needed)

Chapter Four   <u>Helpful Highlights</u>

Completing the information in this section is optional

FIFTH: The following are the names and addresses of the individuals who are to serve as initial Directors.

(Name)

(Street)   NOTE: P.O. Box Addresses are NOT acceptable.

(City)   _(State)_   _(Zip Code)_

(Name)

(Street)   NOTE: P.O. Box Addresses are NOT acceptable.

(City)   _(State)_   _(Zip Code)_

(Name)

(Street)   NOTE: P.O. Box Addresses are NOT acceptable.

(City)   _(State)_   _(Zip Code)_

REQUIRED
Must be authenticated
(signed) by an authorized
representative
      (See Instructions)   Authorized Representative   Date

                            (print name)

                            Authorized Representative   Date

                            (print name)

                            Authorized Representative   Date

                            (print name)

Chapter Four   Helpful Highlights

Complete the information in this section if box (1) (2) or (3) is checked.

ORIGINAL APPOINTMENT OF STATUTORY AGENT

The undersigned, being at least a majority of the incorporators of _____
hereby appoint the following to be statutory agent upon whom any process, notice or demand required or permitted by
statute to be served upon the corporation may be served. The complete address of the agent is

_____
(Name)

_____
(Street)   **NOTE: P.O. Box Addresses are NOT acceptable.**

_____, Ohio
(City)   *(Zip Code)*

Must be authenticated by an
authorized representative

_____   _____
Authorized Representative   Date

_____   _____
Authorized Representative   Date

_____   _____
Authorized Representative   Date

ACCEPTANCE OF APPOINTMENT

The Undersigned, _____, named herein as the

Statutory agent for, _____
, hereby acknowledges and accepts the appointment of statutory agent for said entity.

Signature: _____
                        (Statutory Agent)

Helpful Highlights

The next helpful highlight is the EIN form with instruction that was Step 3 in setting up your nonprofit organization.

Form SS-4 (Rev. 7-2007) Page **2**

Do I Need an EIN?

File Form SS-4 if the applicant entity does not already have an EIN but is required to show an EIN on any return, statement, or other document. See also the separate instructions for each line on Form SS-4.

IF the applicant...	AND...	THEN...
Started a new business	Does not currently have (nor expect to have) employees	Complete lines 1, 2, 4a–8a, 8b–c (if applicable), 9a, 9b (if applicable), and 10–14 and 16–18.
Hired (or will hire) employees, including household employees	Does not already have an EIN	Complete lines 1, 2, 4a–6, 7a–b (if applicable), 8a, 8b–c (if applicable), 8a, 9b (if applicable), 10–18.
Opened a bank account	Needs an EIN for banking purposes only	Complete lines 1–5b, 7a–b (if applicable), 8a, 8b–c (if applicable), 9a, 9b (if applicable), 10, and 18.
Changed type of organization	Either the legal character of the organization or its ownership changed (for example, you incorporate a sole proprietorship or form a partnership)[2]	Complete lines 1–18 (as applicable).
Purchased a going business[3]	Does not already have an EIN	Complete lines 1–16 (as applicable).
Created a trust	The trust is other than a grantor trust or an IRA trust[4]	Complete lines 1–18 (as applicable).
Created a pension plan as a plan administrator[5]	Needs an EIN for reporting purposes	Complete lines 1, 3, 4a–5b, 9a, 10, and 18.
Is a foreign person needing an EIN to comply with IRS withholding regulations	Needs an EIN to complete a Form W-8 (other than Form W-8ECI), avoid withholding on portfolio assets, or claim tax treaty benefits[6]	Complete lines 1–5b, 7a–b (SSN or ITIN optional), 8a, 8b–c (if applicable), 9a, 9b (if applicable), 10, and 18.
Is administering an estate	Needs an EIN to report estate income on Form 1041	Complete lines 1–6, 9a, 10–12, 13–17 (if applicable), and 18.
Is a withholding agent for taxes on non-wage income paid to an alien (i.e., individual, corporation, or partnership, etc.)	Is an agent, broker, fiduciary, manager, tenant, or spouse who is required to file Form 1042, Annual Withholding Tax Return for U.S. Source Income of Foreign Persons	Complete lines 1, 2, 3 (if applicable), 4a–5b, 7a–b (if applicable), 8a, 8b–c (if applicable), 9a, 9b (if applicable), 10 and 18.
Is a state or local agency	Serves as a tax reporting agent for public assistance recipients under Rev. Proc. 80-4, 1980-1 C.B. 581[7]	Complete lines 1, 2, 4a–5b, 9a, 10 and 18.
Is a single-member LLC	Needs an EIN to file Form 8832, Classification Election, for filing employment tax returns, or for state reporting purposes[8]	Complete lines 1–18 (as applicable).
Is an S corporation	Needs an EIN to file Form 2553, Election by a Small Business Corporation[9]	Complete lines 1–18 (as applicable).

[1] For example, a sole proprietorship or self-employed farmer who establishes a qualified retirement plan, or is required to file excise, employment, alcohol, tobacco, or firearms returns, must have an EIN. A partnership, corporation, REMIC (real estate mortgage investment conduit), nonprofit organization (church, club, etc.), or farmers' cooperative must use an EIN for any tax-related purpose even if the entity does not have employees.

[2] However, do not apply for a new EIN if the existing entity only (a) changed its business name, (b) elected on Form 8832 to change the way it is taxed (or is covered by the default rules), or (c) terminated its partnership status because at least 50% of the total interests in partnership capital and profits were sold or exchanged within a 12-month period. The EIN of the terminated partnership should continue to be used. See Regulations section 301.6109-1(d)(2)(iii).

[3] Do not use the EIN of the prior business unless you became the "owner" of a corporation by acquiring its stock.

[4] However, grantor trusts that do not file using Optional Method 1 and IRA trusts that are required to file Form 990-T, Exempt Organization Business Income Tax Return, must have an EIN. For more information on grantor trusts, see the instructions for Form 1041.

[5] A plan administrator is the person or group of persons specified as the administrator by the instrument under which the plan is operated.

[6] Entities applying to be a Qualified Intermediary (QI) need an EIN even if they already have an EIN. See Rev. Proc. 2000-12.

[7] See also Household employer on page 4 of the instructions. Note: State or local agencies may need an EIN for other reasons, for example, hired employees.

[8] Most LLCs do not need to file Form 8832. See Limited liability company (LLC) on page 4 of the instructions for details on completing Form SS-4 for an LLC.

[9] An existing corporation that is electing or revoking S corporation status should use its previously assigned EIN.

Printed on recycled paper

Form **SS-4**
(Rev. July 2007)
Department of the Treasury
Internal Revenue Service

Application for Employer Identification Number

(For use by employers, corporations, partnerships, trusts, estates, churches, government agencies, Indian tribal entities, certain individuals, and others.)

▶ See separate instructions for each line. ▶ Keep a copy for your records.

OMB No. 1545-0003

EIN

Type or print clearly.

1. Legal name of entity (or individual) for whom the EIN is being requested

2. Trade name of business (if different from name on line 1)

3. Executor, administrator, trustee, "care of" name

4a. Mailing address (room, apt., suite no. and street, or P.O. box)

5a. Street address (if different) (Do not enter a P.O. box)

4b. City, state, and ZIP code (if foreign, see instructions)

5b. City, state, and ZIP code (if foreign, see instructions)

6. County and state where principal business is located

7a. Name of principal officer, general partner, grantor, owner, or trustor

7b. SSN, ITIN, or EIN

8a. Is this application for a limited liability company (LLC) (or a foreign equivalent)? ☐ Yes ☐ No

8b. If 8a is "Yes," enter the number of LLC members ▶

8c. If 8a is "Yes," was the LLC organized in the United States? ☐ Yes ☐ No

9a. Type of entity (check only one box). Caution. If 8a is "Yes," see the instructions for the correct box to check.

☐ Sole proprietor (SSN) _____
☐ Partnership
☐ Corporation (enter form number to be filed) ▶ _____
☐ Personal service corporation
☐ Church or church-controlled organization
☐ Other nonprofit organization (specify) ▶ _____
☐ Other (specify) ▶

☐ Estate (SSN of decedent) _____
☐ Plan administrator (TIN) _____
☐ Trust (TIN of grantor) _____
☐ National Guard ☐ State/local government
☐ Farmers' cooperative ☐ Federal government/military
☐ REMIC ☐ Indian tribal governments/enterprises
Group Exemption Number (GEN) if any ▶

9b. If a corporation, name the state or foreign country (if applicable) where incorporated | State | Foreign country

10. Reason for applying (check only one box)
☐ Started new business (specify type) ▶ _____
☐ Hired employees (Check the box and see line 13.)
☐ Compliance with IRS withholding regulations
☐ Other (specify) ▶
☐ Banking purpose (specify purpose) ▶ _____
☐ Changed type of organization (specify new type) ▶ _____
☐ Purchased going business
☐ Created a trust (specify type) ▶ _____
☐ Created a pension plan (specify type) ▶ _____

11. Date business started or acquired (month, day, year). See instructions.

12. Closing month of accounting year

13. Highest number of employees expected in the next 12 months (enter -0- if none).
Agricultural | Household | Other

14. Do you expect your employment tax liability to be $1,000 or less in a full calendar year? ☐ Yes ☐ No (If you expect to pay $4,000 or less in total wages in a full calendar year, you can mark "Yes.")

15. First date wages or annuities were paid (month, day, year). Note. If applicant is a withholding agent, enter date income will first be paid to nonresident alien (month, day, year) . . . . ▶

16. Check one box that best describes the principal activity of your business.
☐ Construction ☐ Rental & leasing ☐ Transportation & warehousing ☐ Accommodation & food service ☐ Wholesale-agent/broker
☐ Real estate ☐ Manufacturing ☐ Finance & insurance ☐ Health care & social assistance ☐ Wholesale-other ☐ Retail
☐ Other (specify)

17. Indicate principal line of merchandise sold, specific construction work done, products produced, or services provided.

18. Has the applicant entity shown on line 1 ever applied for and received an EIN? ☐ Yes ☐ No
If "Yes," write previous EIN here ▶

Third Party Designee
Complete this section only if you want to authorize the named individual to receive the entity's EIN and answer questions about the completion of this form.

Designee's name

Designee's telephone number (include area code)
(   )

Address and ZIP code

Designee's fax number (include area code)
(   )

Under penalties of perjury, I declare that I have examined this application, and to the best of my knowledge and belief, it is true, correct, and complete.

Name and title (type or print clearly) ▶

Applicant's telephone number (include area code)
(   )

Signature ▶   Date ▶

Applicant's fax number (include area code)
(   )

For Privacy Act and Paperwork Reduction Act Notice, see separate instructions.   Cat. No. 16055N   Form **SS-4** (Rev. 7-2007)

States. If you want your organization to be recognized as tax exempt by the IRS, you are required to give us this information. We need it to determine whether the organization meets the legal requirements for tax-exempt status.

The organization is not required to provide the information requested on a form that is subject to the Paperwork Reduction Act unless the form displays a valid OMB control number. Books or records relating to a form or its instructions must be retained as long as their contents may become material in the administration of any Internal Revenue law. The rules governing the confidentiality of the Form 1023 application are covered in Code section 6104.

The time needed to complete and file these forms will vary depending on individual circumstances. The estimated average times are:

	Recordkeeping	Learning about the law or the form	Preparing the form	Copying, assembling, and sending the form to the IRS
Parts I to XI	89 hrs. 26 mins.	5 hrs. 10 mins.	9hrs. 39 mins.	48 mins.
1023 Sch. A	10 hrs. 2 mins.	6 mins.	16 mins.	—
1023 Sch. B	15 hrs. 18 mins.	12 mins.	27 mins.	—
1023 Sch. C	11 hrs. 14 mins.	12 mins.	23 mins.	—
1023 Sch. D	9 hrs. 48 mins.	42 mins.	53 mins.	—
1023 Sch. E	14 hrs. 35 mins.	1 hrs. 9 mins.	2 hrs. 22 mins.	16 mins.
1023 Sch. F	11 hrs. 28 mins.	12 mins.	23 mins.	—
1023 Sch. G	6 hrs. 42 mins.	6 mins.	12 mins.	—
1023 Sch. H	7 hrs. 53 mins.	42 mins.	51 mins.	—

If you have comments concerning the accuracy of these time estimates or suggestions for making these forms simpler, we would be happy to hear from you. You can write to the Internal Revenue Service, Tax Products Coordinating Committee, SE:W:CAR:MP:T:T:SP, 1111 Constitution Avenue, NW, IR-6406 Washington, DC 20224.

DO NOT send the application to this address. Instead, see *Where to File* on page 4.

Helpful Highlights

Last, is the two page form 1023 checklist and page 12 of the application. The current fee is $750. Before you complete the application, always check with the IRS to see what the current filing fee is.

Because of the complexity of the forms, we recommend that you contact an accountant to complete the form properly. An accountant will be aware of the constantly changing updates. There are private agencies that also specialize in completing the form 1023. Be sure to check references, as with any consultant that you hire to complete work.

The entire process to set up a nonprofit, from beginning to end is on the average a year. We have seen as quick as six months.

Once you set up your nonprofit agency with IRS, you are ready to get the Money. Now its time to focus on how to keep the money.

Chapter Four 6. Helpful Highlights

FORM 1023 Checklist
(Revised June 2006)
Application for Recognition of Exemption under Section 501(c)(3) of the Internal Revenue Code

Note: *Retain a copy of the completed Form 1023 in your permanent records. Refer to the General Instructions regarding Public Inspection of approved applications.*

Check each box to finish your application (Form 1023). Send this completed Checklist with your filled-in application. If you have not answered all the items below, your application may be returned to you as incomplete.

☐ Assemble the application and materials in this order:
- Form 1023 Checklist
- Form 2848, *Power of Attorney and Declaration of Representative* (if filing)
- Form 8821, *Tax Information Authorization* (if filing)
- Expedite request (if requesting)
- Application (Form 1023 and Schedules A through H, as required)
- Articles of organization
- Amendments to articles of organization in chronological order
- Bylaws or other rules of operation and amendments
- Documentation of nondiscriminatory policy for schools, as required by Scheduled B
- Form 5768, Election/Revocation of Election by an Eligible Section 501(c)(3) Organization To Make Expenditures To Influence Legislation (if filing)
- All other attachments, including explanations, financial data, and printed materials or publications. Label each page with name and EIN.

☐ User fee payment placed in envelope on top of checklist. DO NOT STAPLE or otherwise attach your check or money order to your application. Instead, just place it in the envelope.

☐ Employer Identification Number (EIN)

☐ Completed Parts 1 through XI of the application, including any requested information and any required
Schedules A through H.
- You must provide specific details about your past, present, and planned activities.
- Generalizations or failure to answer questions in the Form 1023 application will prevent us from recognizing you as tax exempt.
- Describe your purposes and proposed activities in specific easily understood terms.
- Financial information should correspond with proposed activities.

☐ Schedules, Submit only those schedules that apply to you and check either "Yes" or "No" below.

Schedule A Yes_____No_____   Schedule   E   Yes_____
No_____

Schedule B Yes_____No_____   Schedule   F   Yes_____
No_____

Schedule C Yes_____No_____   Schedule   G   Yes_____
No_____

Schedule D Yes_____No_____   Schedule   H   Yes_____
No_____

☐ An exact copy of your complete articles of organization (creating document). Absence of the proper
Purpose and dissolution clauses is the number one reason for delays in the issuance of determination Letters.
- Location of Purpose Clause from Part III, line 1 (Page, Article and Paragraph Number) _____
- Location of Dissolution Clause from Part III, line 2b or 2c (Page, Article and Paragraph Number) or by operation of state law ____

_____

☐ Signature of an officer, director, trustee, or other official who is authorized to sign the application.
  • Signature at part XI of Form 1023.

☐ Your name on the application must be the same as your legal name as it appears in your articles of organization.

Send completed Form 1023, user fee payment, and all other required information, to:

Internal Revenue Service
P.O. Box 192
Covington, KY 41012-0192

If you are using express mail or a delivery service, send Form 1023, user fee payment, and attachments to:

Internal Revenue Service
201 West Rivercenter Blvd.
Attn: Extracting Stop 312
Covington, KY 41011

Chapter Four 7. Helpful Highlights

Form 1023 (Rev. 6-2006) Name: EIN   Page 12

Part XI User Fee Information

You must include a user fee payment with this application. It will not be processed without your paid user fee. If your average annual gross receipts have exceeded or will exceed $10,000 annually over a 4-year period, you must submit payment of $750. If your gross receipts have not exceeded or will not exceed $10,000 annually over a 4-year period, the required user fee payment is $300. See instructions for Part XI, for a definition of gross receipts over a 4-year period. Your check or money order must be made payable to the United States Treasury. User fees are subject to change. Check our website at www.irs.gov and type "User Fee" in the keyword box, or call Customer Account Services at 1-877-829-5500 for current information

1 Have your annual gross receipts averaged or are they expected to average not more that $10,000? no   yes

If "Yes," check the box on line 2 and enclose a user fee payment of $300(Subject to change—see above).

If "No," check the box on line 3 and enclose a user fee payment of $750 (Subject to change—see above).

2 Check the box if you have enclosed the reduced user fee payment of $300 (Subject to change).

3 Check the box if you have enclosed the user fee payment of $750 (subject to change).

I declare under the penalties of perjury that I am authorized to sign this application on behalf of the above organization and that I have examined this application, including the accompanying schedules and attachments, and to the best of my knowledge it is true, correct, and complete.

Please

Sign   _____

Here   (Signature of Officer, Director, Trustee, or other (Type or
print name of signer) Date

 Authorized official)

_____

        Type or print title or authority of signer)

Reminder: Send the completed Form 1023 Checklist with your filled-in-
application. Form 1023 (rev. 6-2006)

Chapter 5

How to Keep the Money

There are ten FAQ (Frequently asked questions) that people ask concerning grants. Everyone would like to receive large amounts of advertised free money. People hear about the billions of dollars available for the asking. This chapter covers the steps needed to get the money and keep it, once you've set up your nonprofit organization.

These are a list of FAQ that people from all walks of life ask:

Question # 1 What is a grant?
Answer: A grant is a sum of money given to primarily a nonprofit organization, except in rare cases like the PELL GRANT, where its given to individuals for educational purposes.

Question # 2 What is a proposal?
Answer: Interchangeable with the word grant. Sometimes referred to as a grant proposal also.

Question # 3 Do you pay grants back?
Answer: No. Grants are given for charitable purposes, usually covering a service to a person whose income falls below the national poverty level. It's a civil service.

Question # 4 Is there a ceiling to the amount of money a nonprofit can receive?
Answer: No. Nonprofit budgets can be extremely small and tight, or have a multi million dollar budget, like the Salvation Army, Boys & Girls Club of America, and the United Way Agency.

Question # 5 Can felons start nonprofits?
Answer: Yes. Some of the most successful nonprofits in the country according to the federal governments Best Practices Publication was started by felons. The number one drug treatment center is located in Maryland, started by two felons. Our Place, a referral and case management agency offering re-entry services, also was funded by two female felons.

Question # 6 Are churches nonprofit 501-C-3 agencies?
Answer: No. A church is exempt from taxes. However, in order to apply for and receive grants, a church must go the extra steps listed in Chapter 4.

Question # 7 Do I need money to start a nonprofit?
Answer: Yes. The filing fees to set up the agency are around one thousand dollars. Check the Sec. of State web site, and the IRS website for filing fee updates.

Question # 8 Is the turn around time for set-up long?
Answer: No. It takes approximately six months to a year for the entire process, from beginning to end. That is not a long time if you weigh out the magnitude of the service you'll be providing to the public.

Question # 9 Do I have to have a board of trustees?
Answer: Yes. The board of trustees is the governing body for a nonprofit organization, per IRS guidelines.

Question # 10 Should I hire a consultant?
Answer: Maybe. There are many deciding factors in whether or not to hire a consultant. If you know of a consultant that offers a free consultation, the best thing to do is to utilize the consultation to ask personalized questions about your project.

There are 10 general components to a grant. For some sections, titles are interchangeable with other words, such as problem statement and program statement. The important thing to remember is that funders are asking, who, why, how, where, when, and back to who again. A grant should cover each and every one of these requests or sub-headings. Some funders require that you fill out the grant on their application forms only, so make sure that you know and understand each guideline of that grant. If you do not attend the RFP session given by the funder, you should call or check the foundations website to get a copy of their rules. The 10 parts of a grant generally are:

1. **The cover page**
2. **Executive Summary**
3. **Problem Summary**
4. **Methodology**
5. **Objectives/Outcomes**
6. **Evaluation**
7. **Sustainability**
8. **Budget and or list of current funding sources**
9. **Budget narrative**
10. **Attachments**
11. **The Cover Page**

This page lists your agency address, phone numbers, fax numbers, website and/or email, contact person for the project, authorized person legally responsible for the grant, the name of the grant you are applying for, and the amount requested. A funder should be able to answer who and where immediately after glancing at the agency cover page.

The contact person and person authorized to sign does not have to be the same person. The contact person is usually the person that wrote the grant. They may be needed to fill in gaps that the funder may need the answer to.

The authorized person is usually the board of director's president. Some funders will accept the signature of the Executive Director along with the board president.

The Executive Summary

This is a concise, one page summary of the agency formation date, the founder, why the agency was formed, the location, and lists the experience of the major players in the project. The executive summary addresses the who, where, and why of it all. In most instances, the summary can be used over and over again, changing only the last 2 lines that usually list the name of the grant being applied for, and the requested amount.

Problem Statement

This is where you clearly describe the problem that you wish to address. A good example of a sentence in a problem statement would be, 'according to the U.S. Department of Justice 2003 Juvenile Justice study, teenagers get into trouble most between the hours of 3:00 pm to 7:00 pm. This is not a local problem. It is a national problem. When you state the problem you are addressing, use concrete data to support your statement. It can be census data or many other sources, but you want to demonstrate what the experts and leaders of the field are saying. It is an organization somewhere that has the data to support your problem statement. A problem statement should be no more than three pages long. Be concise. Verify statistics before you list them. Funders do verify. Some funders are even aware of what the proper statistics are. At the end of the problem statement, the funder should know clearly what you're addressing.

<u>Methodology</u>

After you've clearly listed the problem, your methodology is a detailed account of how you will address the problem. This is the main part of the grant. It answers the who, where, how, and when of your program. An example is, "Mrs. Carol Jones will arrive at the center on Lee Road at 2:30 pm to prepare for the after school program. Children will start to trickle in at 3:00, along with the 5 other part-time program staff. Children will be broke into age-specific groups, and begin planned activities that are listed on the following page. The activities are broken down into groups, with the age of each participant listed. Parents will begin to pick up their children by signing them out with Mrs. Carol Jones, starting at 5:30 pm. By 7:00 pm, the program is concluded, and 30 minutes will be used for clean-up and set-up time to prepare for the next day". That is a brief example of how the program will operate. The more detailed the methodology is, the better. With clear details, the funder is able to visualize your program. The methodology is also where you list the activities of your program. If you have a curriculum design as part of your program, list it also. Any charts relating to the operations of your program also go under this heading. The methodology is commonly three to ten pages. When a funder reads this section, they should understand who is doing what. Also when they are doing it, where they are doing it, and how. Anyone listed in your budget and budget narrative as part of this grant should be mentioned in this section.

Objectives/Outcomes

Your objectives and outcomes are usually six to twenty sentences that are concise and to the point. For example:

> **Objective**- to increase letter grades in school
> Outcome- 35% of children in our after school program will increase one letter grade within the next school year.
> **Objective**- to decrease negative behaviors
> Outcome- 15% of children in our program will become better students in school.
> **Objective**- to increase student proficiency exam results 10% more of our students will pass the proficiency exam than the national average.

These are real objectives and outcomes. They are the kind of things that funders want to hear about. If you do not understand the full concept of outcome measures, I suggest you contact the United Way Agency in your state and see when their next class for outcome measure certification is being offered, or look on their website. The workshop is given to nonprofit staff. It is extremely helpful with training grant writers in outcome measures. The nonprofit sector is highly competitive. In deciding who gets the money, it could be as simple as being able to show some type of results. Put yourself in the place of the funder. Wouldn't you want to give your money to a results oriented program? Of course you would if you had a foundation.

Evaluation

This is a new component of grants. Twenty years ago it was unheard of. Today funders want more accountability and results with their dollar.

Your evaluation tool should be designed specifically to measure the progress of your program. The purpose is to have a measurable outcome.

What our agency did was simple. We designed a short open ended Questionnaire that looked similar to this:

Name: Age: Grade: School:
Subjects:
Current Grades:
(Please attach a copy of report card to survey)

Rate childs behavior
Between one to 10 with   1 2 3 4 5 6 7 8 9 10
Ten being very good   very   very
                           Poor   good

_____   _____   _____
Parents signature   Agency staff signature   Date

Above was filled out at the beginning of the school year. At the end of the school year, we had the parent fill out a new form and date it. The attachment of the report card was a mandatory requirement in order for the parents to register the child into our program. The data from the forms were entered into an Access data base by the program manager to create and manipulate data as part of our monthly and annual reports to funders.

There are hundreds of standard program evaluation forms. How to determine the right tool for your agency is to think about the objectives and outcomes of your program. How do you verify that your program helps children academically? How do you prove that your agency has improved the behavior of your students?

Sustainability

In this section, you are asked to give examples of how you will sustain your program. Many grants are for limited periods of time, such as two or three year funding cycles. Some funders have rules that state that you can apply and receive their money one time only. Other funders will fund you each year, and have a close relationship with the agency staff directors or board members.

There are no guarantees in the funding circle. As a result of social services funding being re-allocated to Homeland Security funding, many steady, secure, established agencies were forced to close their doors. After scaling down staff as much as possible.

Your sustainability plan is not a contract. It gives the funder a glimpse of your management skills. A good manager is also a good planner. An example of a good sustainability plan would read:

Our agency will also target non-traditional funding services and increase our fund-raising projects, such as:

1. The range of our annual campaign.
2. Add a black-tie annual event.
3. Ask board members to approach corporate donors
4. Invest in additional donor lists
5. Recruit parent and community volunteers to solicit funds
6. Have agency car washes, bake sales, and other events to add to the day-to-day funding needed.

The list can go on and on, and should be as detailed as possible.

There are no wrong ideas when it comes to sustaining your agency and keeping your funding base solid. This part of the grant should fit on one page.

List of Current Funding Sources

At the end of your sustainability plan this is a good place to list your current funders, pending funding sources, and potential funders. It is good to form the information into a neat chart or table, on one page, making your sustainability plan a total of two pages. Some funders require a list of your current funders as part of their grant package. Even if they don't, it's good to include it as part of the grant.

Your current funding is money that you currently receive. For example:

Name	Amount	Annual	Start Date	End Date
Department of Health And Human Services	23,000 monthly	$302,000	09/01/1999	on-going
Your pending funding sources could read:	(reported June 2007)			
Cleveland Foundation	Amount		Start Date	End Date
	$300,000	Same	7/1/2007	6/30/2009

Pending funding is funding that you've received the award letter, but not the funding it is also money that has been already ear marked to come to your agency.

Potential funders are grants to be submitted. Funders like to know who the other players are, and what kind of funding you are working on. This also gives the funders a glimpse of the agency management skills.

An example of a list of potential funding is:

Name	Amount	Annual	Start date	End date
Round 27 Block Grant	$10,000 monthly	$120,000	-one year grant-	

Your complete list of funding sources will give the funder a glimpse of the size of your funding base, and who you're requesting funding from. Funders have been known to call other funders and see exactly what component of your agency they fund or intend to fund. Do not be surprised if this happens. This will not interfere with your grant request, but could encourage a funder to change the requested amount, or which component they decide to fund to eliminate double-dipping.

<u>Budget</u>

Often, agencies have a fiscal staff person to complete the budget. However, if you are starting an agency, you may be required to wear many hats. We suggest using a professional accountant to oversee this component. Most agencies cannot afford a full-time accountant. The easiest way to get the most benefit for your agency is to add consultant hours into the grant for accounting services. Also, when selecting board members it is smart to recruit an accountant as a board member. Board members can be paid for any services provided that is part of their profession.

Most accountants serving on the board of the agency will invoice the agency for only 50% of the costs. For example:

Invoice

From: Anderson Accounting Firm

To: ABC Community Center

# of hours	Service	Cost
10	financial statement creation review, and certification	$1,000
	(50% of invoice charged to charity/in-kind services)	
	Total	$1,000
	(in kind) - deduction	500
	Owed -	$ 500

It's a win-win situation. The accountant can write the in kind service amount off of his/her taxes. The agency is receiving professional, needed services for half the cost. The funder is pleased because their interest is protected by using a licensed professional to mind the financial details. An accountant is not mandatory. Many directors are capable of preparing a detailed budget, and familiar with payroll deduction amounts for the state, FICA, and local tax agencies. Some have all the knowledge needed about charge-offs and depreciation costs. A large number of directors do not have the kind of financial savvy needed. It is an individual choice and should be discussed with the Board of Directors. Also, it is rare that an agency has available fees up front to pay an accountant. Therefore, the accountant chosen should be willing to invoice and accept partial payments.

Your budget will vary. It will be based on the amount of money you're asking for, and what components of your program you are requesting money for.

Some funding sources have their own budget forms. This makes it easier to submit exactly what they want.

Some funders do not like more than 25% being charged to salaries. They prefer to spend the bulk of their money on program costs.

Here is a base example of a budget:

Salaries
Consultants
Equipment
Supplies
Overhead
Administration

Salaries are charged to each grant according to the hours that will be spent working on the program. If a staff member is working full-time on the component of the grant, then the full salary can be charged.

An example would be the program manager of a certain component, like after-school programs.

The consultant line is all of the professional services an agency receives in relation to a grant, along with independent contractors offering a service. This line item receives 1099's if over $600 is paid to them during a one year period. This category usually requires a copy of an invoice and/or time sheet to be attached to their payment instrument. The accountant, attorney and other agency contractors also belong in this category.

Remember, we are not accountants or tax advisors. To assure that your agency is in full compliance it is always best to use experts in the field, like in any other business.

The same applies for all of the other categories listed. Have a finance officer review your budget, budget narrative, and line items.

Another tip is to do your homework when it comes to program supplies. Some grants want the program supplies line item separated from regular office supplies. Some funders do not. Some will ask for a detailed list of supplies that combine both office and program items. An example of a few of the program supply items you'll need for a youth after school or summer camp program is:

1. computer printer ribbon
2. boxes of plain paper
3. colored paper
4. colored folders
5. copies (colored & black & white)
6. academic software
7. special skills software
8. cost of lunch for 2 field trips
9. scissors
10. paint
11. crayons

12.   eraserable markers
13.   activity board
14.   video tapes
15.   19' TV/video player

This is the start of a program list for after-school students, K-12, annually. As your program progresses, your supply list will expand. Our program had a boom box and different kinds of music to exercise and relax from, and more detailed art supplies.

In the budget narrative, you detail each line item. Again, an accountant or professional tax advisor will know how to assist your agency with its mission.

Budget Narrative

The narrative is an explanation of each line item. An example is:

Program Manager -   full time, hourly, at $15.00 an hour x 40 hrs. wk, 52 weeks annual-base $31,200.

Program Aide -   Part time, hourly, at $7.50 an hour x 10 hrs. wk, 52 weeks annual-base $3,900.

Each line item must be broke down into amounts to be charged to the grant. Also, for most employees, FICA, social security, state and local taxes have to be filtered into the requested amount unless a funder states that the grant will not cover employee taxes.

If you attempt to complete the budget and budget narrative, be sure to have someone double-check the figures. The budget requested should match the budget narrative to the penny.

<u>Attachments</u>

Every grant has an attachment list. It can be as simple as your exemption letter issued by the IRS, to a complex detailed list, with a check list to make sure everything the funder requests is there.

A few examples of what funders request as attachments are:

1. Job descriptions of employees listed (to see minimum requirements . for job)
2. Resumes of key personnel (to verify experience)
3. Complete agency budget
4. 2 years of Financial Statements (certified by licensed accountant)
5. List of board members with contact addresses and phone numbers
6. Sample of weekly curriculum (programs or training)
7. Letters of recommendation (from mayors, councilmen, constituents
8. Agency brochure
9. Past newspaper clippings or events featured
10. Itemized equipment and supplies list

These are the top 10 additions that may be requested by funders. Even if they do not request them, once you begin to submit grants, it is to your advantage to add them. It gives the funder a clear picture of who you are. A few others might be:

    a.   certificate of good standing (from Secretary of State)

    b.   employee manual

    c.   student handbook

What is important to remember is that funders are people just like you and I. Not machines. Ask yourself, "If I had a foundation and was giving away money to strangers, what would I expect from them?" In answering that question, give as much information about your agency as you can. It may be the deciding factor on whether your agency is chosen or not to receive funding.

Attached is our Helpful Highlights section to help you understand the funding process.

Chapter 5 1. Helpful Highlights

COMMON PROPOSAL FORM
COVER SHEET

The Cover Sheet Summary is to provide the essential data about the organization, the contact person, and the proposal. Please input text in shaded boxes. Complete this form and submit with your full proposal.

Request to: Enter the name of foundation or corporation

Date of Application:

Full Legal Organization Name:			
Address:			
City:		State:	Zip Code:
Website:			
President/Exec. Dir.:		Title:	
Phone #:	Email:		
Contact Person (if different):		Title:	
Phone #:	Email:		

Organizational Information

501(c)(3)? Yes ☐ No ☐ If, Yes, FIN #: 00-1234567	Year established:
If No, provide name of fiscal sponsor (enter organization name and address):	
Total Organization Budget $ Fiscal Yr: Month [select one] Day [select one]	
Total # of Board Members: 0 Total # of staff: 0 Volunteers #: 0	

Organizational Mission Statement (50 words or less):

Brief Description of Organization (75 words or less):

Population Served (25 words or less, include age groups, race & ethnicity, income levels, etc.):

Proposal Request:

Program/Project Name: Enter name; if no name leave blank

Total Program Budget: $	Requested Amount: $	%: 0%
Type of Request: [select from the list]	Grant Period: to	Multi-Year? No

Geographic Area Served:

Priority funding areas of grant maker (indicate how your request fits within the grant maker's strategic interest[s]):

Most recent grants received from this funder:	Amount: $	Date:
	Amount: $	Date:

I hereby verify that the information provided is accurate and honest to the best of my knowledge.

Authorizing signature (President of the Board or Executive Director)   Date

The Budget

The budget for your proposal may be as simple as a one-page statement of projected revenue and expenses. Or your proposal may require a more complex presentation, perhaps including a page on projected support and notes explaining various items of expense or of revenue.

Expense Budget

As you prepare to assemble the budget, go back through the proposal narrative and make a list of all personnel and non-personnel items related to the operation of the project. Be sure that you list not only new costs that will be incurred if the project is funded but also any ongoing expenses for items that will be allocated to the project. Then get the relevant costs from the person in your agency who is responsible for keeping the books. You may need to estimate the proportions of your agency's ongoing expenses that should be charged to the project and any new costs, such as salaries for project personnel not yet hired. Put the costs you have identified next to each item on your list.

Your list of budget items and the calculations you have done to arrive at a dollar figure for each item should be summarized on worksheets. You should keep these to remind yourself how the numbers were derived. These worksheets can be useful as you continue to develop the proposal and discuss it with funders; they are also a valuable tool for monitoring the project once it is under way and for reporting after completion of the grant.

A portion of a worksheet for a year-long project might look like this:

Item	Description	Cost
Executive director	Supervision	10% of salary = $10,000 25% benefits = $ 2,500
Project director	Hired in month one	11 months at $35,000 =$ 32,083 25% benefits = $ 8,025
Tutors	12 working 10 hours per week for three months	12 x 10 x 13 x $ 4.50 = $ 7,020
Office space	Requires 25% of current price	25% x $20,000 = $ 5,000
Overhead	20% of project	20% x $64,628 = $ 12,926

With your worksheets in hand, you are ready to prepare the expense budget. For most projects, costs should be grouped into subcategories, selected to reflect the critical areas of expense. All significant costs should be broken out within the subcategories, but small ones can be combined on one line. You might divide your expense budget into personnel and non-personnel costs; your personnel subcategories might include salaries, benefits, and consultants. Subcategories under non-personnel costs might include travel, equipment, and printing, for example, with a dollar figure attached to each line. Overhead, or indirect costs, is important to include because projects do not exist in isolation. Funders may have policies regarding the percentage of overhead they will allow in a project budget, if they allow it all.

Support and Revenue and Statement

For the typical project no support and revenue statement is necessary. The expense budget represents the amount of grant support required. But if grant support has already been awarded to the project, or if you expect project activities to generate income, a support and revenue statement is the place to provide this information.

Chapter 5 2. Helpful Highlights

COMMON PROPOSAL FORM
PROJECT & ORGANIZATION BUDGET SUMMARY

Organization Name   Enter Organization Name Here
Federal ID #
Fiscal Year End   12/31/2007

	Enter Program/Project Name Here				
	This Request	Total Project Budget	% to Total Income	Total Organization Budget	% to Total Income
Income Sources					
Government Grants	-				
Foundation and Corporate Grants	-				
United Way	-				
Individual Contributions	-				
Earned Income	-				
Interest Income	-				
In-Kind Support	-				
Other Income	-				
Total Income	-	-			
Expenses					
Salaries and Wages	-				
Employee Benefits and Taxes					
Total Personnel Costs	-	-			
Depreciation Expense	-				
Equipment Rental & Maintenance	-				
Food Costs	-				
Fundraising/Development Expenses	-				
Insurance Expense	-				
Marketing/Advertising	-				
Postage and Delivery	-				
Professional Development	-				
Professional Fees	-				
Rent and Occupancy	-				
Supplies and Materials	-				
Telephone Expense	-				
Travel Expense	-				
	-				
Miscellaneous Expenses	-				
Total Non Personnel Costs	-	-	-		
Total Expenses	-	-	-		
Excess of Revenue Over Expenses	-				

Enter Footnotes Here

Chapter 6

More Money

There are hundreds of nonprofits set up annually. The agencies that make it are the ones that have a diverse fundraising strategy.

In this Chapter we are going to talk about four common fundraising strategies used by nonprofits throughout the country. The first is the most simple.

AGENCY CARE WASH

To have a successful car wash all you need are lots of rags, a connection with a faucet, buckets, cleaning solution and washers. Here are a few suggestions:

1. Have your clients or students you serve bring in rags. Yes. That simple. Like companies collect cans of food for food drives, have a barrel set up to collect donations of rags. Bag them up in clear plastic garbage bags. You can never collect too many. If you have an enormous amount, store them for the next car wash.

2. There are two ways that you can obtain your cleaning supplies. You'll need about one hundred dollars to make each thousand. The

first way you can obtain the supplies you need (i.e. buckets, cleaning solution, a car vac) is to go and buy the items you need. The second way is to take your tax exempt letter to one or two of your neighborhood stores and have one or two stores donate what you need. List the donors as sponsors of the car wash, which assists them in advertising their businesses. Many neighborhood stores will gladly give a small amount like one hundred dollars for a good cause. It doesn't have to be a store that has the actual goods. A grocery store, dry cleaners, restaurant, and any other neighborhood store can be a potential partner in your mission. It is important to contact the business in advance in person, or by phone. Planning is very important in hosting a fundraiser. For a car wash, if it unexpectedly rains, try to reschedule, but always offer the service promised. If you have posted flyers and handed them out, simply change the date on the flyer, and at the location you listed on the flyer, have clear signs stating the new date and time.

3. Get kids from the high schools and churches in your community. You can do this by meeting with the church leaders or secretary, and the guidance counselor at the high school that is responsible for community service. There are senior high school students that have to complete community service hours as part

of their graduation requirement. The senior students are expected to contact a nonprofit organization, hospital or nursing home to fill out a form to complete their community service hours. By doing this, seniors benefit by fulfilling their graduate requirements, and your agency benefits because you have a pool of good, voluntary workers. It's a win-win situation. If you are not familiar with neighborhood schools, churches, and other businesses change that. Network with them immediately. They will come in handy in assisting you in completing your agency mission. At a basic $10 a car, your agency can easily gross two thousand dollars (or more, depending on how many kids you have) in a short period of time. Also, car washes can be a lot of fun on a sunny morning.

BLACK TIE EVENTS

The second form of fundraising to consider is hosting a black-tie event. It can be a dinner, dance, or both. The easiest way is to have your funders as the guest of honor, or a potential sponsor.

Here are a few suggestions:

1. Solicit a sponsor of your black tie event. Expect to ask them for five to ten thousand dollars. The money will cover the place where you plan to have the event, and a Dee Jay. Also the cost of

purchasing the menu items, and paperware that included tablecloths, napkins, etc. The amount of money you ask for will depend on the number of people you expect to attend. If you do not have an event planner on your board of directors, have one of your board members locate one. There are some board members that are experts at organizing fundraisers. Strategically choose your board to have a wide array of directors that include a few constituents. Also, it is important that you send a flyer to the city newspaper to list your black-tie events. Every newspaper usually has a section for weekly or monthly events. There is usually no charge for nonprofit organizations to be put on the calendar.

2. Charge enough for the tickets to see a profit. How much do you charge for a ticket? It's a wide range of what an acceptable price is for a ticket. Make sure that all costs have been factored in, because once you get your tickets and special invitations printed, there is no turning back to change or rearrange things. $75 is an average scale for a black tie dinner and dance. You will have many people that will not come, but will buy tickets to support your fund-raiser. Also, each board member should sell twenty tickets for the agency. Staff members should also chip in to sell tickets. Appoint one staff person and one board

member to monitor ticket sales and money from both ends. The board member assigned is responsible for signing out tickets, collecting money from the other board members, and keeping clear account of the money. The staff person that accepts the assignment should be management or administrative staff with strong organizational skills. The staff person collecting the money and monitoring ticket sales should coordinate regularly with the board staff assigned to the event.

3. Proper set-up and organization of your event will determine the success of your venture. If you have no one in charge, the event can turn into a disaster. Nobody will know where exactly the money is, how many tickets have been sold, or who is not carrying their end in ticket sales or turning money in.

Many halls and food suppliers or caterers will accept a third or half of the total price as a down payment, and expect the balance at a later date. This balance usually comes from ticket sales. If you are not organized, when it comes time for the final phase of your black-tie event, it may not come together as planned. Planning and organizing is everything in successfully pulling off a black tie event.

ANNUAL CAMPAIGNS

The third type of fundraiser is your agency annual campaign.

A suggestion of when to begin your annual campaign for your agency is after you've obtained your permanent exemption status from the Internal Revenue Service.

If your original application is accepted and approved by IRS, you receive a "temporary" 501 C 3 status. The top right hand corner of your exemption letter will state the date that you can apply at the earliest for permanent exemption status. The date listed is usually three years following your set-up and approval date.

In the context of your exemption letter, the IRS will give you clear instructions on when and how to apply for your permanent status. It is not a complex process. In general, you have to inform the IRS of your current board, their contact information, funders, copies of 990 tax filings and other agency information that's generally at the fingertips of an active nonprofit agency.

Once your agency receives your permanent status, you're ready to put together your strategy for an annual campaign. A good way to come together as one thought pattern and focus on the task is by having a retreat. The retreat should host your officers of your Board of Directors, all administrative staff, and any other key management and direct service staff that will be involved directly in the agency annual campaign.

Your annual campaign is once a year, every year. There is no set month to have your agency campaign. However, check and see when the major players have theirs, and then schedule yours on a different time schedule. Your agency annual campaign will give you a good source of unrestricted contributed income. When you set out to raise money, set your goals realistically.

Your strategy is to build a pool of regular annual donors who will commit a predictable base of support. The majority of individual donors give their first contributions to an agency through its annual campaign. Your annual campaign should run about six weeks. If a donor has not returned the mailing envelope with their donation within six weeks, they are usually not going to. There are a few donors that will trickle in after the official ending of the campaign, but the bulk of the money will come in within two weeks of receiving the solicitation.

Annual campaigns can have hundreds, thousands, and even tens of thousands individual donors. The agency board usually solicits their area of specialty. Construction workers usually can access lists of construction companies. Bankers can obtain lists of banks and their key personnel. Medical staff can usually get an agency listing of employees. Even if it's a phone roster, it can be used to make phone contacts and increase donors. A well connected Board of Directors is a well funded agency.

Your campaign envelope should have a high end solicitation envelope, asking for one thousand, or five hundred, or a fill in amount. Your standard envelope should always list an amount. Each year, raise slightly the amount you asked for last year. The primary goal of an annual campaign is to raise money. The secondary goal is to raise public awareness of your agency.

This is where you profile your agency in press releases. An example of a press release is:

<u>Sample</u>
ABC Community Center kicks off annual campaign today. Friday, September 1.

The goal for the year is one million dollars. The center will kick off the Campaign at Randall Mall with Sherry Walker, Operation Director, leading a march through the mall. Center T-shirts will be given to the first 50 hundred dollar donors. Last years campaign raised $800,000 under the leadership of Kecia Green. Ms. Walker noted that the current target has some added, "stretch factor".

ABC Community Center offers after-school programs, little league, summer camp, meal on wheels for the elderly, and daily recreational activities for children and adults. Call, write and e-mail Sherry Walker.

Your biggest expense for your agency campaign is going to be postage.

During this time, it's also feasible to request employee contributions. A few corporations and foundations will also support your campaign. Some specifically list this as one of their funding areas, and help to fund the expenses incurred during an agency campaign.

An endowment or capital campaign is also needed. These type of efforts cushion the agency and should be a concentrated administrative project. A capital campaign is also called a Special Purpose Campaign. There is no limit to what amount you ask for during an endowment or capital campaign. That depends solely on the giver that you're soliciting.

If your agency expects to benefit from estate planning, it is best to work directly with a banker or even better, have a banker on your board of directors. Bankers work in the bank directly with estate planners for the bank. Estate planners decide what charity will get the clients money. Bankers know first when a client is considering donating a large amount of their money to charity.

Once your agency builds a substantial amount into your endowment, then the Board of Directors should begin to look at some sound investments. Your Board of Directors should already have knowledge of the business consultants needed to move your agency ahead. If not, recruit new board members that are knowledgeable in the areas that you'll need guidance.

To be clear, how Estate Planning works is an expert is assigned a number of clients that have a large estate with lots of capital. An estate planner coordinates with the owner of the estate where the money will be spent. If an agency can win over just one large donor from an Estate Planner, that will provide the cushion an agency needs.

Most donations that come from an estate is a six-figure donation.

Remember, do not leave your constituency out. Some of the targeted population that you serve has a wide base of friends, church members and family members. You can never do too much soliciting of potential donors for your agency.

Following is Helpful Highlights, with sample figures to help you understand the fundraising process.

Chapter Six 1. Helpful Highlights

For the Fiscal Year_____

Annual Campaign Figures

Division	Prior Year	Losses	Net Available	Estimated Increases	Actual Net Result
Corporations	$30,000	$1,000	$29,000	3,000	$32,000
Foundations	5,000	N/A	5,000	N/A	5,000
Trustees	10,000	2,000	8,000	1,000	9,000
Individuals	50,000	2,000	48,000	3,000	51,000
Misc.	800	N/A	800	200	1,000
	$95,000				$98,000
					(Forecast)

Chapter Six 2. Helpful Highlights

Sample Operational Budget &
Current fiscal Year Projection

OPERATING EXPENSES $1,600,000

	(less)		
19%	Earned Income	300,000	
			$1,300,000
	(less)		
09%	ENDOWMENT INCOME	150,000	
	SPECIAL GIFTS 7 GRANTS	350,000	
			500,000
50%	BALANCE TO BE REFUNDED		$800,000
100%			

Chapter Six 3. Helpful Highlights

Sample Donor List

Foundations	Public Charities
The Barra Foundation, Inc	California Healthcare Foundation
Birmingham Foundation	McCormick Tribune Foundation
The Bush Foundation	Messouri Foundation for Health
The Dan Foundation	The Pew Charitable Trusts
Deer Creek Foundation	Rockefeller Family Fund
Doris Duke Charitable Foundation	Youth Foundation, Inc.
The Ford Foundation	Fannie Mae Foundation Fund
The Freeman Foundation	Washington Area Women's Foundation
Gates Family Foundation	The Wolpert Fund
The Hearst Foundation	The Sherwick Fund
The Robert Wood Johnson Foundation	The True-Mart Fund
The Kresge Foundation	Chisholm Memorial Fund
The Rockefeller Foundation	Candelaria Fund
The Wallace Foundation	The Chris Tensen Fund
Anonymous (20)	Gara Fund

Corporations	Individuals
Alcoa Foundation	The England Family
Altria Foudnation	The Castle Family
American Express Foundation	The Ferguson Family
Avon Foundation, Inc.	The Bechtel Family
The Coca Cola Company	The Moran Family
IBM Corporation	The Dreyfus Family
The Merck Company Foundation	The Turpin Family
J.P. Morgan Chase & Co.	The Walker Family
Morgan Stanley	The Green Family
Motorola Foundation	The Cohen Family
Pfizer Inc.	The Krieble Delmas Family
State Farm Companies Foundation	The Greenwall Family
The U.P.S. Foundation (UPS)	Samuel H. Kress Family
Wells Fargo Foundation	Andrea Young Family
The Xerox Foundation	The Zellerbach Family

Chapter 7

Money for Churches

The Faith Based Initiative was introduced by President Bush in his 200th State of the Union address. The initiative encouraged partnerships with churches, and promoted the idea of churches receiving funding from all funding sources. Before President Bush initiative churches were not the targeted population to receive funding, although many churches throughout the country did receive money.

President Bush received public criticism because of the required separation of church and state. However, the Faith-Based Initiative forged on.

Churches were required to follow the regular steps listed in Chapter 4 of this book to become a nonprofit agency that received grant money. Churches are not automatically able to receive grants. Most pastors and church members do not know this. We will explain it.

Per IRS regulations, churches, synagogues, temples and mosques do not have to file Form 1023 for 501-(C) (3) tax exempt status. Churches are already considered to be a tax exempt agency. However, if churches wish to receive a determination letter that recognizes them with a section 501 (C) (3) status, and specifies whether contributions to them are tax deductible, they must file form 1023.

In simple words, to get grant money, churches have to follow the steps in Chapter 4, to set up a nonprofit. An example of how it works is: Progressive Baptist Church can set up Progressive Development Corporation, or Progressive Community Center. The grants would come in under the nonprofit corporation entity of the church, not directly to the church.

Can the same staff and directors that run the church also run the nonprofit corporation? Yes.

Can different people run the corporate end? Yes.

Can there be shared staff and the responsibility split between the church and the corporate end of the church? Yes.

There are two key requirements for an organization to be exempt from federal income tax under section 501 (C) (3). The agency must be organized and operated exclusively for one or more exempt purposes.

1.   Organized as a corporation, and permanently dedicate its assets to exempt purposes, and

2.   Operated to further one or more of the exempt purposes stated in its organizing document.

In order to get the money, churches must organize as corporations. You can collect tithes forever and never fill out a form 1023 or incorporate, and still be the strongest church in your neighborhood if you do not wish to apply for grants.

Generally, when determining whether a section 501-(C) (3) religious organization is a church, IRS will consider characteristics attributed to churches, and facts and circumstances of each organization applying for public charity status. To be considered a church, a congregation or other religious membership group is required. For more detailed information, see IRS Publication 1828. The practices and rituals associated with your religious beliefs or creed must not be illegal or contrary to clearly defined public policy.

Part of the criticism that President Bush received about the merging of church and state was that churches lacked business ethics and public accountability. We believed in the church as a conduit to wrap around services of community members. However, the adversaries of the Faith-Based Initiative had a strong point. Most churches do not have a strong sense of accountability. If the church needed a roof, and the pastor held $20,000 roof repair money in his hand, the roof won over the meal-on-wheels or other social programs. What is wrong with that? It's illegal! When you apply for grant money in order to offer a specific service to the community, the money must be spent accordingly. Churches struggled with this.

J.U.M.P. Inc. formed a faith based collaboration under the supervision of Dr. Rev. Charles Britton during this time. The Faith-Based collaboration was a group of churches bound together by one program agent, and one fiscal agent. How it worked is Churches would register for the collaborative by filling out a standard three page form, designed by the Board of Directors of J.U.M.P. Inc. Also, the title was approved for the Faith-Based component of J.U.M.P. Inc. It was named unanimously I.J.N. Foundation. I.J.N. Foundation stood for the words, "In Jesus Name." It was set up as a DBA (doing business as) and fictitious name, under J.U.M.P. Inc.

This was a very difficult collaboration. The main challenge was to assist old-fashioned ministers to change their thought processes. The mind-set of some of the ministers was that to receive grant money was the equivalent of "begging." Another common barrier in the way of successfully partnering churches with grant money was getting church administration to be complete team players. Rev. Britton had an excellent idea in partnering churches to fill the gaps in services throughout the city and African-American communities. Rev. Brittons idea preceded president Bushes initiative, but did not gain momentum until President Bush pushed churches to the head of the funding receivers.

Reverends were not the easiest partners. They wanted everyone to join the board, donate your time, or do everything for free in the "name of the Lord." Many churches missed out on the billions of dollars being given out all over the country due to the listed barriers. Churches that had a strong business constituency or business leadership were the beneficiaries of the Faith-based Initiatives.

Rev. Moss led the example of Best Practices by leading his Cleveland, Ohio church to the point of excellence. He incorporated training programs, job readiness, welfare to work compliance, and many other wrap-around services, provided by his charitable corporation.

COMMUNITY PARTNERSHIPS AND INITIATIVES

Also during the Faith-based Initiative, the Community Reinvestment Act of 1977 (CRA) took on an upswing in popularity.

The CRA was enacted in 1977 to prevent red lining and to encourage banks and thrifts to help meet the credit needs of all segments of their communities, including low and moderate-income neighborhoods. The act extended the longstanding expectation that banks would serve the convenience and needs of their local communities.

The law provided a framework for depository institutions and community organizations to work together to promote the availability of credit and other banking services to underserved communities. The Faith-based Initiatives also promoted community collaborations and new projects in the inner city. Money by way of low-income loans became readily available for participants of the CRA and the Faith-Based Initiative. Housing also topped the list of needed obstacles to success in our inner cities. Development Corporations such as Famico's Foundation built the organization to a multi-million dollar housing development agency. Almost 30 years later, Famico's Foundation is still the biggest housing service agency in Cuyahoga County. Jim Williams had a passion. As the executive director of Famico's and a construction supervision by trade, he made it work. Famico's Foundation came together in a partnership with the churches under the CRA, and the Faith-based Initiative.

The Community Affairs Department along with the Faith-based Initiative came together to form the same common goals, which were:

- To provide training and technical assistance on effective strategies for community development, formation of community development corporations, community development bank offices in the inner city, investing in community service projects, community partnerships with churches, and neighborhood businesses all equally involved in reversing the plight of urban neglect in our neighborhoods.

- Conducting tailored one-on-one consultations with national banks, assisting these institutions in identifying opportunities and resources available to support community development.

- Sponsoring conferences, round table discussions, and workshops for the exchange of information and ideas, among lenders, community groups, and government officials.

- Develop publications and web-based resources on innovative approaches through community collaborations, to serve underserved communities.

It was a big ticket. There were national conferences in L.A., California, Orlando Florida, and local meetings springing up at all major Universities in large cities. During the throws of the Initiative, President Bush had a section of the White House website established to contact his committee leaders of the Faith-based Initiative.

The Initiative included Churches. The role of the church has always been to act as a safe haven and solace for communities. Dating back centuries, the church fed the hungry, visited the sick, comforted the mentally ill and physically afflicted, and gave a sound foundation to families that joined their congregation. Over the years, participants have increased and decreased in repetitive cycles, but the services offered remain constant.

President Bush and Rev. Britton believed that the church should be a pro-active nucleus in solving community problems. Both men believed that the church could offer unique, non stereotypical services to a large, divest constituency. The Faith-based Initiative bottomed out due to millions of social services dollars being re-allocated to the Homeland Security Fund. In Ohio alone, the Cuyahoga County Commissions funding was cut from 129 million, to 30 million the first year following 911. Many agencies that relied on county funding were devastated. Many went under.

The agencies that survived were the ones that had a diverse funding base that included foundation and corporations. Agencies with a profit component, such as daycare and subsidized housing were able to overcome the sharp, deep budget cuts of county, state and federal funding.

That's why it is important to keep up with government initiatives. Also, it helps to review the federal government's current and projected fiscal budget. How this can help you is to give an idea of how much funding is being allocated, and to whom. Funding trends change annually. You can find out what current initiatives are by visiting the White House website, HUD (Department of Housing and Urban Development), the Department of Education, and all other federally governed agencies. All have websites listing current initiatives. The list of these federal agencies can be found in Chapter 1 of this book.

Because of the limited amount of funds available, during President Bush second term, the Faith-Based Initiative converted informally to the Re-Entry and Ready-4-Work Initiative. The governing agency of the funding became the U.S. Department of Labor, Center for Faith-Based and Community Initiatives.

The Prisoner Re-Entry Initiative was designed to help strengthen urban communities and assist ex-prisoners re-entering the community through an employment-based program that incorporated housing, mentoring, job training, and other services. The Prisoner Re-entry Initiative was designed to draw on the unique strengths of faith-based and community-based organizations, and rely on them as primary partners. At the national level, many federal and corporate partners participated in the Partnership for Prisoner Re-entry to provide guidance and support for the Initiative.

Under this current Initiative, 30 agencies throughout the country were awarded funding. The October 3, 2007 list can be viewed following this chapter contents under Helpful Highlights. During the first year of program operations, the 30 grantees collectively provided 43,495 services to 6,442 participants and placed 3,378 participants in employment.

To contact the supervision of this grant initiative, contact:

Employment and Training Administration
U.S. Department of Labor
Frances Perkins Building
200 Constitution Avenue, NW
Washington, DC 20210
1-877-US-2 JOBS
www.doleta.gov

Former President Bill Clinton's initiative focused on welfare to work programs and Youth after School Programs. J.U.M.P. Inc. received funding from the county under both of former President Clinton's Initiatives, and serviced both populations. Most Initiatives only last three years. Ready-4- Work ended in 2006.

To help you understand Initiatives better, President Bush began his campaign in 2004 with the Faith-Based Initiative. The Faith-Based Initiative merged into the Ready-4-Work Initiative. The Ready 4 Work Initiative was a 22.5 million dollar program, that was created to assist faith-based and community programs that provided mentoring and other transition services for men and women returning from prison. Ready 4 Work was jointly funded by the U.S. Department of Labor, the U.S. Department if Justice, and a consortium of private foundations.

Many times you do not have to re-invent the wheel. Best practices is a federal website and office that tracks agencies receiving federal funding and reviews them for Best Practices. The review is based on standard criteria. The agency selected is featured on the Best Practices website and rated. The staff at the Best Practices office is very helpful. Once they find out what type of agency you are interested in surveying, they place you in contact with one of the model agency staff. There are also some funding available to visit other agencies throughout the United States, if you are willing to pay part of the expenses. The deciding factor in determining the amount of money they give you is how much funding the Best Practices office has available at the time of your request.

To offer the best services, take the time to review what national agencies like yours are doing, and find out simultaneously what some of their obstacles are, and how to overcome them. It only cost your time and the benefit is priceless. Funders love to see data from the top agencies that is providing the services you are asking them to fund. Also, it displays strong management and administrative skills on your part.

An example of a good agency to contact to get an overview of re-entry services that work is the grantee, in East Harlem N.Y., called Exodus Transitional Community, Inc. The agency has served over 1,500 men and women generally returning from prison. 75 to 80 percent of Exodus participants do not return to prison, compared to a national recidivism rate of almost two-thirds, Executive Director, Julio Medina reported. What are their key practices and processes? That is what re-entry programs around the world should be asking. However, many agencies do not take the time to complete their homework on who the competition is in their field. It saves months of reinventing the wheel on all aspects of your agency. The $300 million prison re-entry initiative is currently at the top of the list for 2007. What will the next Initiatives promote? The public may not know in advance, however, as an agency director it is important that you know and understand initiatives, their purpose and how they work.

Where churches fit into the current funding cycle is as community partners. Churches with a corporate structure has always been able to enjoy a large array of funding diversity.

Tithes are important. However, often the Church does not have enough to do the work in the community that it would like. That is where forming a nonprofit corporation to off-set costs can come in handy. What is important is to make sure that the church has someone with a strong business sense, and skills. Accountability is where a lot of churches fall short. Grants can offset the high over head of church expenses by allowing the church to charge-off a percentage of space and utilities used for program use.

If a church has a nonprofit agency component, some of the expenses of the nonprofit can be offset by using church members as volunteers for some of the agency duties. An example would be a church with a large professional constituency. If you have accountants, attorneys and business consultants, why go outside the church? These people can donate 50% of their billable hours to the nonprofit agency sector of the church by charging only 50% in fees. It's a win-win situation for churches to establish nonprofit corporations.

J.U.M.P.'s Faith-based component titled I.J.N. Foundation solicited grant money for a large church collaboration. The incoming grants were divided among the registered partners. There needs to be more collaboration formed like that. Churches usually have a basement to offer some type of services to their community.

ROLES OF FELONS IN NONPROFIT

Last, but equally important is the role of felons in your agency. The first thing to consider is whether or not your agency will hire felons. If so, what is the minimum amount of time, if any, that felons have to wait before their last conviction. There is an employee bonding available, as well as tax credits for companies that are willing to hire felons. Make sure it is part of your application process to ask, and screen employees.

Wendy's Restaurant uses the benefits of employee tax credits by hiring felons on a large scale. How the credit works is that your tax liability decreases if you hire felons. A company with a $17,000 tax liability to I.R.S. can eliminate the large amount of taxes owed by employing 10 felons throughout the year, if the tax credit allowed is $1,700 per new hire. Check federal and state guidelines.

The credits, limitations, and other guidelines vary, and are constantly updated. There is a minimum amount of time that the employee has to work in order for the employer to be eligible.

Often, people ask if felons can start a nonprofit and receive grants. Yes they can. The Board of Directors of a nonprofit agency is legally responsible for the employees of the agency, including the Executive Director. If the Executive Director violates the law, the Board of Directors can be sued. If your Board of Directors is not governing the agency properly, the agency is in trouble, and not following the guidelines established by the I.R.S.

Felons throughout the country start and implement some of the most innovative, high-end service delivery nonprofits in the country. Angel Tree that issues toys to the children of prisoners was started by a felon, after she witnessed the need while serving a 15-year prison sentence. Angel Tree started out with a X-mas tree, and a few donated toys. Now the agency is operating in most prisons throughout the country. Angel Tree partnered with churches and other nonprofits to broaden their base of children that could be reached. The only requirement is that one of the parents of the children be in jail. The Prison Fellowship Program started an international pen pal club. The owner was also in prison and saw that there was a need for prisoners to correspond with the outside world to keep hope alive while doing time. Our Place in Washington D.C. was started by two female felons. It is an agency that assists with housing, and connects released female inmates to a large pool of services. Who would know what services are needed better than inmates returning to society? In the case of the above listed agencies, experience was the best teacher.

If your agency is offering services to elderly citizens and children, felons may also have some restrictions due to a federal approved house bill restricting felons from working with elderly and children. The rules may vary from state to state, so check with the state attorney general. Also, if your church or agency is facilitating a BINGO game or other games of chance as fundraisers, there may also be restrictions. The state attorney general governs the laws of charitable fundraising. It is important to be aware of currents laws governing your agency.

Can convicted felons sit on the Board of Directors? Yes, if the board is properly set up, there will be at least one constituent chosen from the population served. This person should be given equal consideration in the major decision making of the agency, as well as serving or committees. Your neighborhood based board member(s) will keep you grounded on what's going on with your agency that is not public knowledge. People talk. Committees share opinions and criticisms. You want at least one community liaison serving as one of your agency board of directors. Often, this person may be a felon, or may not be. Felons cannot run BINGO games in some states, so make sure that you know the rules in order to strategically position your Board of Directors to work for you.

If you do decide to hire felons, check with websites

to see what other services may be available to you. There are programs that will pay part of a felon's salary as well as carry some of the risk of hiring felons by offering supervision of felons while employed in your agency. More than 10 percent (30 million) people in America are convicted felons. Discuss with your Board of Directors what your agency position will be for hiring felons or using felons as volunteers or board members.

The Helpful Highlights section of this Chapter will give you the I.R.S. definition of churches, the 30 grantees that received the prisoner re-entry grant, with an actual two page news article.

Chapter Seven 1. Helpful Highlights

The characteristics generally attributed to churches are as follow:

1. A distinct legal existence
2. A recognized creed and form of worship
3. A definite and distinct ecclesiastical government
4. A formal code of doctrine and discipline
5. A distinct religious history
6. A membership not associated with any other church or . . denomination.
7. Ordained ministers ministering to the congregation
8. Ordained ministers selected after completing prescribed courses of . study
9. A literature of its own
10. Established places of worship
11. Regular congregations
12. Regular religious services
13. Sunday schools for the religious instruction of the young
14. Schools for preparation of ministers.

For more information, see IRS Publication 1828

Chapter Seven 2. Helpful Highlights

October 3, 2007
Prisoner Re-Entry Initiative Contacts
Service Provider

	City	State	Contact phone
The Primavera Foundation, Inc.	Tucson	AZ	520-623-5111
Arizona Womens Education and Employment Inc	Phoenix	AZ	602-223-4333
Metro United Methodist Urban Ministry	San Diego	CA	619-285-5556
Allen Temple Housing and Economic Development Corp.	Oakland	CA	510-409-5831
Mexican American Alcoholism Program, Inc.	Sacramento	CA	916-394-2320
Fresno Career Development Institute Inc.	Fresno	CA	559-498-7155
The Empowerment Program	Denver	CO	303-320-1989
Community Partners in Action, Inc	Hartford	CT	860-566-2030
OIC of Broward Co. Inc.	Ft. Lauderdale	FL	954-535-2178
The Directors Council	Des Moines	IA	515-697-5704
The Safer Foundation	Chicago	IL	312-922-4767
The Church United for Community Development	Baton Rogue	LA	225-408-3380
Odyssey House Louisiana, Inc	New Orleans	LA	504-821-9211
Span, Inc.	Boston	MA	617-423-0750
Episcopal Community Services of Maryland	Baltimore	MD	410-467-1264
Oakland Livingston Human Services Agency	Pontiac	MI	248-451-1770

	City	State	Contact phone
St. Patrick Center	St. Louis	MO	314-802-1953
Connections to Success	Kansas City	MO	314-333-4497
Career Opportunity Development	Egg Harbor City	NJ	609-965-6871
The Doe Fund, Inc	Brooklyn	NY	212-628-5207
Goodwill Industries of Greater NY and Northern NJ, Inc.	Astoria	NY	973-481-2300
Urban Youth Alliance International Inc.	Bronx	NY	718-402-6872
Talbert House	Cincinnati	OH	513-751-7747
SE Works Inc	Portland	OR	503-772-2302
Connection Training Services	Philadelphia	PA	267-977-3853
WABC Central City Comp. Comm. Center	Houston	TX	713-579-2728
Goodwill Industries of San Antonio	San Antonio	TX	210-924-8581
Urban League of Greater Dallas and North Central Texas	Dallas	TX	214-915-4604
People of Color Against AIDS Network	Seattle	WA	206-322-7061
Word of Hope Ministries, Inc	Milwaukee	WI	414-447-1965

Chapter 8

Money for Housing

This chapter has three components of explaining money for housing. The first part of the chapter covers information to assist in setting up a halfway house. The second part is to help the reader under the overlapping differences in transitional and subsidized housing. And last, direction to get free money to purchase a house and rehab it.

Halfway House Setup

Many individuals want to set up a housing program to help different targeted populations. It is an excellent idea. There are several business structures that can be used. The house does not have to be a nonprofit. If your house is not set up as a nonprofit you must still obtain approval locally. In most cities, this is done by creating a short proposal and presenting it to the city council meeting. There you will find out if the community advocates with you, or if they oppose. If the city you are attempting to set up in has a neighborhood block watch or similar neighborhood club, we suggest that you present your proposal to the president of the neighborhood watch club first, and attempt to win him or her over. That way you will also find out how receptive the neighborhood is to your project. If you are able to go into the city council meeting with a signed letter of support from the neighborhood watch program, its smooth sailing.

City council will request the standard inspections, blueprints of the space, and an occupancy permit before you open the doors, but tend to work with you if the neighborhood is not opposed.

Make sure that you are prepared to answer difficult questions at the city council meeting. For example, if you want to open up a halfway house for ex-offenders as a re-entry program, how will you safeguard the community from further crimes? That's always a big question. Also, if you're considering a re-entry program, you have to consider what, if any crimes committed will be restricted from applying as residents. Many programs will not accept offenders convicted of rape. Some will not take arsonists. Some will not take medication-dependent mental health patients. It's important that you do your homework and know the targeted population well that you are attempting to serve. You can do this by reviewing other programs in the city on the internet, or the data governing the population you wish to assist by providing housing.

Funding Your Halfway House

There are several levels of funding available to you to fund your program. Here is just a few:

1. The county you open in
2. The state you open in
3. Rehabilitation and Correction
4. Mental Health Agencies
5. Corporations
6. Local funding
7. Department of Agriculture (federal)

The county offers an application that will pay a per diem for housing programs that assist them in their mission. One of their missions is to provide self-sufficiency to youth that turn 18 years old, while in the custody of the county foster care program. There are thousands of youth that have been in the foster care program for different periods of time that must leave the program at the age of 18 years old. The question that is posed is "Where do they go?" You can't place them on the streets. The reason why a large number of youth turning 18 years old in the foster care system is because there is no family member or personal support system to take them in.

The county will pay on the average $134 per day, per child. The amount may fluctuate higher or lower. The purpose of the county funding is to cover staffing, overhead, and program tools to move the youth to self-sufficiency, where they can be able to find a place and live on their own. Cuyahoga County Commissioner Dimora, and Jane Campbell, before Mrs. Campbell became Mayor were sticklers for finding and funding housing initiatives for this population.

The population does come with barriers, therefore be prepared to explain to the community how you will prevent youth from hanging out in areas of the neighborhood. That has always been a major concern. The second similar population that warrants a per diem payment from the county is juveniles that have been extracted from their homes for a multitude of reasons. Some are already part of the juvenile justice system. Some are not. It's still an intricate process to manage a house full of juveniles. If you have lived with teenagers on any level, you know that managing 10 to 15 under the same roof is a 24 hour job. The financial benefits are good if you open up a halfway house, but make sure you understand the obstacles in dealing with your targeted population.

Licensing by the state is a different application than the county, with a different per diem pay per client. State licensure usually requires a few additional compliance requirements in staffing, and structure. You may not have needed full handicap accessibility for county license, but it's a state requirement in most states. They do have state funding assistance available to help you bring your home into compliance, most of the time. To get the money, you have to be in total compliance, and pass the state inspection.

The entire process for county and state licensure takes approximately one to two years, depending on where you live. What deters many people from starting these types of programs is the financial strain they present. Not many people can afford to have a property sit empty with no income stream, while going through numerous local, county and state inspections. However, if you can bare the financial pinch, the benefits are worth it.

The federal department of agriculture will provide food stamps to purchase food, or a food voucher, if you agree to offer at least one meal to the population you intend to serve. This involves a separate series of inspections from the Department of Health and Safety and the agency governing public food preparation in your area. Proper ventilation, temperatures on the refrigerators used to store food, and the types of refrigeration and temperature preparation all have to be assessed and monitored annually in order to access this pot of assistance. Many houses offer a continental breakfast that consists of cold cereal and/or donut, milk and juice, a sandwich and chips with a piece of fruit for lunch, and one hot cooked meal. Your menu has to be prepared by a licensed dietician.

These challenges are not difficult. Consulting with an agency offering the same or similar type of services you wish to offer is the easiest way to get into compliance, and to access the needed financial resources to run a good program. With children, you have to offer some type of meals. With adults you do not.

The department of rehabilitation and correction offers re-entry funding to pay for housing for their clients leaving prison. A standard amount is $700 a month, for a halfway house that is mainly to provide a bed to sleep in out of the natural elements. Most people that fall up under the re-entry classification are required to obtain employment. You can charge a weekly or monthly fee from employed clients to subsidize the costs of running the program. This cost is usually a percentage of the tenants' income. Before you begin your housing program, it is important that you establish the policy governing the program. It is also a good idea to have each new tenant read and sign a copy of the program rules and house policy upon entry. When you begin to locate clients for your house, you will be asked over and over again what the rules of your program are. For re-entry programs, you can mail or fax the application or rules of your program directly to the Chaplain of the prison. Every jail and prison has a Chaplain that is on the staff full-time or at minimum a part-time Chaplain. The Chaplain will post your program rules. The Chaplain has a general idea of who needs housing assistance. Also, it is not uncommon to have the contact information for your program read at the Sunday Church Service with "new announcements". Because of the large number of people being released from prison monthly, there will never be a shortage of clients for your housing program.

If you have a house for males that is a mixed population unit, the shelters are also a way to identify employed clients looking to move out of the shelter, but not ready to take on the full responsibility of an apartment.

Funding Diversity for your Halfway House

There is more than one strategy for recruiting funding sources for your halfway house. We've explained to you a few of the different sources of funding. It is also a good idea to have a mixed population unit. You create that when you reserve a few beds or slots for re-entry persons, a few for homeless persons, a few for veterans, and a few for mental health clients that need little or no supervision. An example is if you have a house with 16 beds, and you dedicate four beds to each of the four funders listed above (veterans, re-entry, homelessness, and mental health), what happens is four different agencies will be providing funding to your program. Each funder has different paydays and schedules to send out checks. With a diverse funding stream you do not put all your eggs in one basket.

The challenge is having to deal with different agencies that require separate compliance reports, and managing different populations. Diversity is not for everyone. There are some homes that are content in serving and specializing in one population of clients. You as the owner and designer of your program must decide what is right for you.

Housing for the Elderly

If your target population is age 55 and older, then you are eligible for the pools of money that is available to provide housing and services to the elderly. There is money available for everything ranging from unassisted living, to setting up full care nursing homes. The Department on Aging funds programs across the United States.

Many elderly persons become displaced each year due to divorce, loss of income, or loss of employment. There are services available, but there is also a demand for a larger supply of services for the elderly. Unfortunately, there is not enough of a supply in this country to meet the demands of poverty for the young or the elderly.

Most of the same rules and steps apply if you want to provide housing for the elderly. You have to go through your city, inspections, and licensure for certain components of care to the elderly.

As suggested for the other halfway house programs in this chapter, the best way to get a feel of what you need is to visit a program similar to the one you wish to begin.

Halfway Houses can require the least amount of staffing if you choose a general, independent population to serve. A house manager that adopts the dual role of tenant is sufficient for adults with no special care needs.

Next, we'll explain how transitional and subsidized housing works.

Transitional Housing

The four types of Transitional housing are:
  1. Emergency shelters
  2. Halfway Houses
  3. Three Quarter-way housing
  4. Temporary Housing

The public often uses the names of transitional housing interchangeably. The identifying difference is the amount of services offered, coupled with the expected length of time a participant will stay. Housing programs are set up in America to decrease the level of homelessness and despair, and as an aid to combat poverty. Poverty is a mass problem of the American culture. Many Americans are living at or below the National Poverty Level. The National Poverty Level income table is created and established by the federal government. In order to be able to access services that are free or partially subsidized and funded by the government, individuals and families must meet the income criteria standards.

If properties have a rent subsidy to keep rents lower, the property agent can tell you how to apply, or either you can apply directly at one of the neighborhood development corporations or affiliates. If there is a rent subsidy, there is a property agent that will accept applications. If the applicant can pay the rent and meet other requirements, e.g. have a reasonable credit history, and some type of income, even if it is a fixed monthly income, then the applicant can be placed on the waiting list.

Rent subsidies keep rents lower. If the right size unit is available applicants must have (1) an income at or below the maximum established income limit for the unit, (2) document income information and (3) agree to pay the established rent. You do not apply directly to HUD for this type of housing, nor does HUD manage housing. When an agency has a rent subsidy or any other kind of assistance, that is because they have submitted a grant proposal to HUD and applied for the money to help subsidize the properties. The reason why a property owner would do this would be in order to address the homeless situation. The grant proposal would state that in the program or problem statement.

This chapter covers a wide array of housing directives, from how to apply if you have nothing, to obtaining grants for housing programs. When you apply for a grant as an agency for any of the transitional housing programs or subsidized housing programs you, have to clearly state how you will guarantee that the clientele served falls within the income guidelines. A large percentage of the funding sources for these types of programs come from taxpayers dollars. As a taxpayer, income earner, or a person responsible for making monthly rent or mortgage payments, would you accept that you were paying your co-workers or bosses rent? No. That is not a pleasant thought.

If you are an applicant for a low-income housing program, one of the first things you are required to present that is part of a mandatory check-list is proof of income. Income tax statements, paycheck stubs, copies of fixed income checks such as welfare and social security income, are all a part of the income verification process.

Federal grants that address homelessness originate from the Department of Housing and Urban Development for the most part (HUD). For the year 2005 which is listed as FY 2005, (meaning funding year 2005), there was $1.244 billion awarded nationally for the continuum of care programs that include the transitional housing programs and subsidized housing programs.

Emergency Shelters throughout the country was awarded $159 million. A sample of Ohio funding for housing is listed in the helpful highlights section of this chapter.

In each area of the country, there are residency preferences for the owner of the property to consider. Residents are defined as:

1. Applicant who work in the jurisdiction
2. Applicants who have been hired to work in the jurisdiction, or
3. Applicant who are expected to live in the jurisdiction as a result of planned employment

If a person is an active participant in an education or training program located in a residency preference area, these individuals should be given preference because they are preparing themselves for the job market, thus, boosting economic development of the neighborhoods.

Owners of properties are not allowed to hold units open because of residency preference. If there is a waiting list, procedure states that the next individual or family waiting for help should be admitted.

If you are applying for a grant, you must set up your screening criteria uniformly for all applicants to prevent discrimination and avoid fair housing violations. It is just as important to keep out drug trafficking and other criminal activity. Unfortunately, these things can go hand-in-hand if tenants are not screened and monitored.

Owners must establish standards that prohibit admission of:

1. Any household containing a member who was evicted in the last three years from federally assisted housing for drug-related criminal activity. The reason for this prohibition is that if a person has already been evicted from a program, like the projects or Metropolitan Housing Authority, HUD does not want to continuously rent to the person that has already violated the policy.

There are four levels of transitional housing programs. Transitional Housing programs are not created with the goal to live there permanently. The objective is to transition individuals with obstacles back into main stream society by providing a safe haven to keep them off the streets.

To qualify for these programs, you have to be considered homeless. Homeless means that you do not own a place of your own. If you live with your girlfriend or boyfriend, and the lease is not in your name, you are considered homeless by legal standards set by the federal government. If you live with your parents, siblings, or any other family members, you are considered homeless. Your home is somewhere that you cannot legally be put out of without going through a court eviction process. Clients have stated that they were not homeless due to living with several family members or mates. Until an emergency occurred, these clients were safe from being on the streets. Each individual case is different in determining homelessness, but the legal guidelines are the same throughout the United States.

Emergency shelters are set up for situations where it is necessary to get into an environment of immediate safety. Safety from domestic violence, the natural elements such as hurricanes and winter conditions, fires, or being abruptly removed from your environment. Emergency shelters are not set up for long-term residency. The usual stay is a few hours to an overnight stay.

One of the way emergency shelters work is by allowing a person to stand in line in front of the business establishment or shelter facility. We have all witnessed people standing in line late evening in front or around a church, waiting to get in. The line was comprised of either clients waiting for emergency shelter or a food kitchen. A food kitchen is also a popular way that churches are able to offset their overhead cost.

Minimal personal items are allowed due to the lack of storage room in an emergency shelter program. Some emergency shelter programs offer meals. Many do not. Because there is an abundance of homeless people living in the United States, there is a limit to the number of clients that are admitted daily. A person entering into a homeless shelter program is not required to pay. There is little or no privacy, and usually set up in dorms or cubicles in order to provide service for the largest number of persons.

If you are considering setting up an Emergency Shelter program, there are several things to consider. Staffing can be offset by using volunteers. Also, overhead cost can be partially cut by partnering with your neighborhood church, if they have a large enough finished basement or space to place clients of an emergency shelter.

For all the transitional housing programs, if you are setting up, there are preliminary steps that are standard across the board. Your business has to be approved on the local or city level, county level, and state level. To begin the process, after finding a physical location, you can call the city inspection department and schedule an appointment to have the unit inspected. The city inspector will require the blueprint of the building, a certificate of use stating that the property was set up for business use and not residential use, and proper ventilation, parking and multi-entrances along with enough exits in case of fire. When you apply at the local level they will explain to you each step, and give you a checklist. Each city is different, although the basics are the same.

Once you are fully approved by the city that you plan to place your emergency shelter, you will be issued an occupancy permit by the city. Your county may have a few other requirements, and so might your state. The main reason why you would be required to complete several levels of inspections would be due to receiving grants and public donations. Receiving taxpayers' dollars raises the bar of accountability.

Emergency Shelters have the least amount of direct service hours, and minimum need for administrative staffing.

The second component of transitional housing is the halfway house. Halfway Houses cater to a certain population. The two main areas are re-entry and mental health clients. The most obvious difference between an emergency shelter and halfway house is the amount of time the client is expected to stay at the program. The standard programs are set up ranging from a week to six months. Halfway houses standardly do not offer a lot of wrap-around services. A client is allowed to go to work, sometimes pay a set amount of their pay, and sleep there. Halfway houses are used to transition inmates and mental health clients back into main stream society. Halfway means that a person is half way out of the situation they came from, and has one foot on solid ground. When you set up a halfway house, your goal should be to assist a person with that mission. Halfway houses usually get residents from referrals.

The third type of transitional housing is three-quarter way housing. This type of housing is usually up to a year in length. It is almost the same as halfway houses except that three quarterway housing usually offers some type of counseling, drug testing, or other transitioning services. Many also offer some type of meals, and have a set of guidelines to be followed. The type of services offered and the length of stay is what determines whether or not you are applying for or setting up a three quarterway house. The word furlough house is also interchangeable with the word halfway house, and three quarterway housing. Where the word furlough originated from is when inmates in state and federal prisons used to be able to participate in furlough programs from prison. The state prisons would release inmates around a year before their sentence expired, in the event of good behavior. The furlough house was governed by a full staff of counselors, case managers, and supervisors. If you messed up, you were immediately sent back to prison. The opportunity was considered a furlough from prison, and you were reminded regularly that if you did not comply in any way, you would immediately be returned to the prison that you were furloughed from. Programs are seldom called furlough houses today, although some are ran with the same principle, such as CCA's that are now a part of the federal sentencing system CCA stands for Community Corrections Agency. The average stay a CCA is usually six months. The sentencing judge determines if and when an inmate returns to prison for a violation.

With the influx of prisoners rising at an alarming rate, the demand for CCA's is growing. If you are considering opening up a CCA, the rules are set and standard across the board. There is not a lot of room for creating your own innovative programming, but there is funding available. Check websites and also visit the nearest CCA in the city that you wish to set up in, or any city that you might be visiting to see how the places are set up. CCA's accept state and federal prisoners, and also accommodate both male and female inmates upon release. Many also have a drug treatment component that is in partnership with the local courts and authorities, depending on bed availability.

Along with the drug treatment component, CCA's have a disciplinary component with them. There is a standard procedure for violations that must be followed, that includes contacting the U.S. Marshalls, the probations departments, or the courts when a person is in violation of any of the rules that is part of the CCA's programming. The job of enforcing the rules is one of the things to consider in setting up a CCA. All things are not for everyone. Some people would love to have this duty as part of their agency description, and others would not. It is important that you understand exactly what is required on all levels when you set up your transitional housing program.

Temporary housing is the least restrictive of all four of the types of transitional housing programs. The usual programs last no more than two years. During the two years that a client lives in a temporary housing setting, they can be supervised by a counselor or other staff. This type of housing usually has some type of phases that you begin with a rigid arrangement, later phasing up to less restrictive living arrangements. Temporary Housing is used to transition persons to permanent housing. This type of housing was used at the Hitchcock Center for Women in Cleveland, where women that were being released from drug treatment was allowed to live in a temporary setting, inside of the building where they received treatment for a period of no more than two years, and also apply for permanent housing. Once a woman completed the treatment program, they lived in one of the rooms classified as temporary housing, applied for Section 8 Horizons for the Homeless program, and received a voucher for housing. This type of housing starts out with daily restricted movement, and an enforced curfew. In the later phases, women are allowed to go home for the weekend and holidays to spend time with their families.

Most traditional housing that is classified as temporary housing has a phase-up component. This type of housing was designed with standards that assist clients with multiple barriers, such as drug addiction, prison re-entry and mental health issues. Each barrier has a different funding pot.

Transitional housing aiding drug addiction can tap into HUD funding, but also SAMHSA (Substance Abuse Mental Health Administration), both state and county substance abuse governing agencies such as ODADAS which is the Ohio Drug Abuse and Drug Addiction System, and foundation funding. Foundations and corporations list their focus in their annual report as well as in the Foundation Directory. It is good to check with the funder to determine if their focus has changed or shifted. It is not uncommon for a foundation to focus on substance abuse one year, then welfare to work training programs the following year. It happened with the shift of priorities within the Clinton administration when William Clinton was president. For a few years, many foundations and corporations main focus was on assisting society with some of the overwhelming substance abuse issues. During the Clinton administration, many foundations changed their focus. Once the statistics came in, many funders decided that their money would be better spent helping youth mentoring programs and welfare-to-work clients. Funding for substance abuse programs was drastically cut. That happens. It is important to follow funding trends and cycles.

How you do that is by using the trade magazines and tools. The main source is the Chronicle of Philanthropy, and the Federal Register. Both will keep you up to date on funding cycles and upcoming Grant initiatives.

The previous pages cover short-term, temporary housing programs ranging from emergency-shelters to two year temporary housing programs. Each of these programs were designed to transition individuals from homelessness to safety. Each of the transitional housing programs were classified according to the amount of time clients utilize the services.

Subsidized Housing

This type of housing is long-term, and extends from the single person to families. The main difference between subsidized housing and a house or apartment that is not subsidized is the method in which the unit is obtained. For unsubsidized housing, you simply find the house or apartment you want, and if you meet the owners' requirements, it's yours. The common name is standard housing.

Subsidized housing is governed by a nonprofit or bureaucratic agency. Also you have to meet income guidelines in order to be eligible for any type of subsidized housing.

The most common type of subsidized housing is the projects, or the proper name is Metropolitan Housing Authority. If a city doesn't have an office then the county usually does.

Housing projects are built for large numbers of low-income families. A project may have small houses built to look alike to save cost, row houses, or apartment buildings. Some low-income projects have a mix of all three.

Local governments persuade large insurance companies and other developers to build housing projects. The companies that agree to build receive special tax deductions on the property.

An example of this is Fresh Meadows in New York City. The project was built by the New York Life Insurance Company. Within the 174 acres, there are approximately 11,000 people in 3,000 units. The down side of living in a housing project is the congestion. The positive side is the low rent. You pay rent according to your income. A family can pay as little as one dollar. Imagine clearing up all income except for a dollar in rent! The demand for public housing exceeds the supply.

The federal government, through HUD, provides funds for local housing authorities to operate public housing. The government pays the difference between the cost of the housing and the rents that low-income families pay.

As a result of the U.S Housing Act of 1937, a low-income family is charged no more than 30% of their income for rent. The second kind of subsidized housing is the Section 8 program. It works like the Metropolitan Housing Authority program, and is often ran by the same office. The Section 8 program is also funded by HUD.

The major difference in the main component of the Section 8 program is that with Section 8, HUD provides a cash allowance given monthly to landlords to allow low-income people to be able to rent private owned housing. Like all other programs for low-income families, the tenant is required to pay no more than 30% of their income for rent, and the government pays the rest. For example, if a unit is valued at $1200, and a low-income tenant has a monthly fixed income of $900, the tenant will be required to pay $300 a month, and the government pays the owner of the property $900 a month. For the landlord, the pro of this agreement is that they will receive the rental payment from Section 8, the first of the month like clockwork. The con is that some of the tenants that receive Section 8 do not care for the property as the owner would.

The pro for the tenant is that they are able to avoid the congestion of public housing areas. With Section 8, any unit that the landlord agrees to accept Section 8 is funded. The con is that in some of the suburbs there are other hidden costs that families may not be able to afford. To date, there are over a million private housing units receiving Section 8 rent subsidies from the government.

As part of the Section 8 program, they have a program called Horizons for the Homeless. HFTH is designed to aid a specific population of people. Mental Health, AIDS, Substance Abuse, and SRO (Single Residence-Occupancy) clients. In order to access the HFTH program, the client has to apply through a nonprofit organization. The nonprofit applies for the grant from HUD in order to provide Section 8 certificates to the population that they serve. An example is Hitchcock Center for Women in Cleveland. Nora Thomas-Griffin solicited the grant for the program. She and I applied for a federal grant from HUD that provided Section 8 vouchers for women graduating out of the residential treatment program.

The agency that applies for the grant from HUD assumes the responsibility to screen, place and monitor the housing units, vouchers and the clients. That is one of the main components of the HFTH Section 8 program.

SRO's are usually multiple dwellings such as apartment complexes that have been rehabbed and then purchased by a nonprofit organization. The agency that owns the dwelling determines the guidelines for the building. With a regular Section 8 voucher, the cash value has portability. You can use it anywhere, and even transfer to a different city or state as long as the state you wish to go to has a HUD housing program.

With an SRO unit, there is no portability. You are applying for a particular unit in an apartment building. The building usually has a property manager on site. SRO's were designed specifically for single people. Many of the clients that meet the eligibility for an SRO are referred from a government program, with a few barriers that prevent the client from achieving standard mainstream living arrangements.

There is no time limit that a person can live in the projects or in a Section 8 unit. However, subsidized housing was designed in order to move low-income families to self-sufficiency. The purpose of charging lower rent is to aide families in being able to save, go to school, or make it through life crisis such as loss of a spouse by divorce or death. However, due to on going economic poverty levels and factors causing poverty remaining consistently the same, subsidized housing is considered a way of life for many.

The third type of subsidized long term housing is the Shelter Care Plus program. It may have different names in some cities. The program is sponsored by the Eaton Corporation in the State of Ohio.

Shelter Care Plus has an enforced time limit. The program funding covers the security deposit, and rents for up to five years. The program helps people that are experiencing barriers when applying for standard housing. The Shelter Care Plus population includes the same constituents as the HFTH program. Mental Health, Substance Abuse, and AIDS persons are the beneficiaries of the Shelter Care Plus program. The main difference in rules of the Shelter Care Plus program that distinguishes it from the HFTH program is that after five years, the recipient is cut off of the rent benefits. There are no extensions, and no exceptions. I've witnessed a person coming off the Shelter Care program that positioned themselves to purchase a home. While receiving free rent for five years, they were able to save money, build up their credit file, raise their credit score, graduate from a skilled licensed practical nursing program, gain meaningful employment, and move on with their lives. On the other hand, I've also observed a client that was not ready to move into a life of self-sufficiency.

As a result of her struggle with the AID's virus, her health was a constant challenge. Self-sufficiency was a difficult goal for her to obtain. She ended up returning to the daily hustle and bustle of living in a homeless shelter.

The Fourth type of housing is a similar subsidized, long-term program with a five year term limit, funded by the FHA (Federal Housing Administration) called the purchase program. The FHA provides mortgage insurance to the nonprofit agency that develops and manages the housing project.

Famico's Foundation is a development corporation established in the city of Cleveland by Mr. James Williams. He wrote the grants and solicited the funding for the housing component. The first component of his program was a restricted five year residency of newly developed properties. Like the Shelter Care Plus program, after five years a family had to vacate the premises. The long-term home purchase program was also a development project of nonprofits. The rent is subsidized, and the loan was guaranteed by FHA. We have all viewed the single family, new construction homes.

A client has to apply at one of the neighborhood development corporations or their equivalent. The income requirements are higher than other subsidized housing programs, and an acceptable credit report is required. The reason is that the family is expected to purchase the home under a 15 year mortgage plan. There are other costs such as water and sewer that the tenant has to pay.

The main difference between standard housing purchases and these type of housing purchases through a nonprofit is that the nonprofit acts as property manager. The agency regulates the mortgage payments, and checks on the physical condition of the property regularly. The reason is because the nonprofit agency that developed the property is the owner. If the tenant defaults on payments, the property goes back to the nonprofit to attempt to place an eligible family in the home. That is why the more secure an applicant's economic status is, the better their chances of becoming the deed holders of the property.

The first part of this chapter dealt primarily with explanations of how transitional and subsidized housing programs operated.

The last part of this chapter will deal with the business of setting up or purchasing housing.

Is there free money to purchase a house or rehab a house? That's a question that is asked often. The answer is for an individual there is not a funding source that will purchase a house. There are one dollar auctions in most cities. My Uncle Jessie purchased his first home for one dollar from a local Cuyahoga County Sheriff's sale, held in Cleveland Ohio, at 10:00 am, every Monday morning at the Sheriff's Department. They have Sheriff's sales all over the country.

The houses that are sold for one dollar are usually gutted out, or structures that have barely survived a fire or flood. The units always need total rehab. The reason why they are sold for one dollar is to assist in neighborhood beautification. If a residential area has a house that experienced a fire, the entire street looses value of their homes. When the market value is calculated, if there are substandard houses aligned with standard housing, the market value goes down. If a neighborhood eliminates the substandard housing from the equation, the housing value remains fairly constant.

When a person buys a house for one dollar, the party is able to receive some type of assistance in rehabbing the house. This can be grants, low interest loans, or both. What is given out depends on what is available in the city that the purchase of the house was made.

The main requirement for receiving financial assistance to rehab these type of properties is that you do it in a timely manner. The deadline dates are given to you by the funder. That is what is meant in the statement heard often that you can get free money to purchase and/or rehab a home.

A second type of grant that is available that does not have to be paid back is a neighborhood beautification grant. This is where a nonprofit in the area applies for a grant for a specific project. An example would be a home repair grant. If a resident needs a new roof, their house painted, or any other project that would aide the neighborhood in looking better or up to par with the other properties, then they can get the grant money. There is usually a limit on funds, and there is also an income restriction. The reason why an income restriction is implemented is because the free money is designed to help families that may be struggling at the time, or on a fixed income. Elderly homeowners are generally included in this type of funding.

The procedure is usually to bring the agency managing the program three beds, and they will pick the best contractor. The contractor must be registered with their office. The agency will allow you time to get your contractor of choice registered with the city if they are offering the best price.

City LandBank

If a person calls the city office that they live in, they can get the number to the sheriffs sales, and the time to purchase discount or one dollar houses. The city information staff will also give them the number or agency that governs the funding to rehab the discounted units. The local department of development is also a good place to check to see what type of grant money is available and to review their landbank list. The landbank is a list of vacant land, abandoned, and foreclosed properties owned by the city. There are standard procedures established to obtain a property from the landbank, but there are some financial incentives available. The city administrators benefit when a condemned unit is taken and rehabbed to be brought up to the standard of the current market value in the neighborhoods. Like the discounted sheriff sales properties, many of these units have a fire or flood damage, condemned or gutted, and may need total rehab. An agency or individual has to weigh out what is the most cost-effective way to obtain property. There are grants available to aide in purchasing and rehabbing these types of units.

An agency or nonprofit entity can obtain properties in the landbank for free. That is right. Free. And then free money to assist in rehabbing the property. We see churches popping up in major cities on every other block. How this occurs is that an individual forms a church using the IRS 1023 exemption application. The same steps are followed that we listed previously in Chapter Four—How to get money.

When an individual sets up a church, the organization becomes a tax exempt charitable religious agency. IRS has set up guidelines that are minimum requirements to gain this tax exemption status. Using a church as your legal structure, your agency can get properties free out of the landbank, and convert them instantly into churches. That is one of the reasons we have so many churches in major cities.

Storefronts, converted houses, office buildings or warehouses are turned into churches. In Ohio we even have a previous movie theatre that has been converted into a church.

At the end of this chapter, The HELPFUL HIGH-LIGHTS will display a current income limit chart, photos of public housing. A 2004 and 2005 News Release from HUD.gov, Characteristics of Transitional Housing, and Emergency Shelter Grants.

Chapter Eight I. Helpful Highlights

<u>News Release</u>

HUD No   For Release
(312) 353-6236 x 2666   Tuesday
www.hud.gov/news   July 13, 2004

BUSH ADMINISTRATION ANNOUNCES
MORE THAN $117 MILLION TO STIMULATE
ECONOMIC AND HOUSING IN OHIO
Grants benefit Barberton, Cincinnati, Hamilton, Hamilton
County, Middletown and State of Ohio.

COLUMBUS, OH – Communities in Ohio
received more than $117 million in federal funding to
stimulate local economics, produce more affordable
housing and help the homeless individuals and families.
The funding will also help house and serve individuals
with HIV/AIDS and will provide downpayment assistance to lower income families.

The funding announced today will help lower
income individuals and families living in Barberton,
Cincinnati, Hamilton, Hamilton County, Middletown
and in smaller communities throughout Ohio.

"This Administration is committed to promoting
economic development and job growth, increasing the
supply of affordable housing, and helping our most

vulnerable neighbors," said Housing and Urban Development Secretary Alphonso Jackson. "These funds will serve as a catalyst for low-income families trying to cross the threshold into homeownership and reinforces our commitment to rebuilding entire communities."

For the past 30 years, HUD's *Community Development Block Grant* (CDBG) Program has awarded over $100 billion to state and local governments to target their own community development priorities. CDBG is one of HUD's oldest and most popular programs. The rehabilitation of affordable housing has traditionally been the largest single use of the grants although CDBG is also an important catalyst for job growth and business opportunities. CDBG funds are distributed by formula around the country based on community population, income levels, poverty rates and the age of its housing stock.

HOME (Home Investment Partnerships Program) is the largest federal block grant to state and local governments designed exclusively to produce affordable housing for low-incoming families. Since 1992, more than 600 communities have committed to produce nearly 785,000 affordable housing units, including almost 300,000 for new homebuyers purchasing their first home. In addition, over 100,000 tenants have received direct rental assistance.

The American Dream Downpayment Initiative (ADDI) aims to increase the homeownership rate, especially among lower income and minority house-holds, and to revitalize and stabilize communities. ADDI will help first-time homebuyers with the biggest hurdle to homeownership: downpayment and closing costs. The program was created to assist low-income first-time homebuyers in purchasing single-family homes by providing funds for down-payment, closing costs, and rehabilitation carried out in conjunction with the assisted home purchase. Information about this program is available on the Internet.

Emergency Shelter Grants (ESG) help local communities to meet the basic shelter needs of homeless individuals and families. These grants also provide transitional housing and a variety of support services designed to move the homeless away from a life on the street toward permanent housing. This block grant program, with more than 1 billion HUD awards by competition, helps thousands of local homeless assistance programs to help those who would otherwise call the streets their home.

HUD'S *Housing Opportunities for Persons with AIDS* (HOPWA) grants are distributed based on the number of AIDS cases reported to the Centers for Disease Control and Prevention. The grants provide rental assistance and support services to individuals with HIV/AIDS and their families. In addition, the HOPWA program also helps many communities develop strategic AIDS housing plans and fill in gaps in local systems of care. A stable home environment is a critical component for low-income persons managing complex drug therapies and potential side effects from their treatments.

HUD is the nation's housing agency committed to increasing homeownership, particularly among minorities; creating affordable housing opportunities for low-income Americans; and supporting the homeless, elderly, people with disabilities and people living with AIDS. The Department also promotes economic and community development as well as enforces the nation's fair housing laws. More information about HUD and its programs is available on the Internet at www.hud.gov and espanol.hud.gov.

#

Community	Grant Type	Amount
Barberton	CDBG	$898,000
Cincinnati	CDBG	$16,103,000
	ESG	$596,391
	HOPWA	$550,000
	TOTAL	$17,249,391
Hamilton City	CDBG	$1,831,000
	HOME	$490,360
	TOTAL	$2,321,360
Hamilton County	ADDI	$193,586
	HOME	$1,443,003
	TOTAL	$1,636,589
Middletown	CDBG	$799,000
Ohio State Program	ADDI	$2,791,270
	CDBG	$57,083,300
	ESG	$3,147,441
	HOME	$30,816,335
	HOPWA	$1,041,000
	TOTAL	$94,879,346

Chapter Eight 2. Helpful Highlights

News Release

HUD No. 05-125OH   For Release
(312) 353-6236 x 2666   Tuesday
www.hud.gov/news   January 25, 2005

BUSH ADMINISTRATION ANNOUNCES RECORD 41.4 BILLION TO HELP HUNDREDS OF THOUSANDS OF HOMELESS INDIVIDUALS AND FAMILIES

HUD funds will support 145 programs in Ohio

COLUMBUS – Housing and Urban Development Secretary Alphonso Jackson today announced Ohio will receive $68,455,503 to provide shelter and care for persons and families without a home of their own. The funding to Ohio is part of more than $1.4 billion announced nationwide-the largest single commitment of federal funds supporting an unprecedented number of local projects on the front lines of caring for people who might otherwise be living on the streets.

Jackson announced the funding at a local homeless center in Los Angeles with California Governor Arnold Schwarzenegger.

"President Bush is deeply committed to supporting our most vulnerable neighbors and today

I am pleased to reconfirm that commitment," said Jackson. "This unprecedented level of funds will go directly to those on the front lines, who work tirelessly everyday to bring an end to chronic homelessness, and who provide services to the many individuals and families without a home of their own."

This is the fourth consecutive year HUD is providing record funding for homeless assistance and is part of a larger federal strategy being embraced by a growing number of state and local communities to end long-term or chronic homelessness.

HUD's funding is provided in two ways:
- *Continuum of Care* grants provide permanent and transactional housing to homeless person. In addition, Continuum grants fund important services including job training, health care, mental health counseling, substance abuse treatment and child care. HUD funds will assists the Continuum of Care in Akron/Barberton/Summit County ($2,727,863), Canton/Massillon/Alliance/Stark County ($2,234,386), Cincinnati/Hamilton County ($10,202,604), Cleveland/Cuyahoga County ($18,748,577), Columbus/ Franklin County ($6,927,718), Dayton/Kettering/ Montgomery County

- ($$5,320,910), Toledo/Lucas County ($3,434,948), Youngstown/Mahoning County ($1,873,312) and in the Balance of the State of Ohio ($9,997,065).
- Emergency Shelter Grants convert buildings into homeless shelters, assists in the operation of local shelters and fund related social service and homeless prevention programs. Emergency Shelter Grants in Ohio total $6,988,120.

Combined, HUD's Continuum of Care and Emergency Shelter Grant programs will provide critically needed funding to more than 4,400 local programs in all 50 states, the District of Columbia, Puerto Rico, Guam, and the U.S. Virgin Islands. As a result, more than a quarter-million persons will receive the housing and services they need to become self-sufficient. For a more detailed local summary of the funding announced today, visit the Internet.

More than $1.2 billion in Continuum of Care grants are awarded competitively to local programs to meet the needs of their homeless clients. Continuum grants fund a wide variety of programs-from street outreach and assessment programs to transactional and permanent housing form homeless persons and families.

Emergency Shelter Grants are allocated based on a formula to state and local governments to create, improve and operate emergency shelters for homeless persons. These funds may also support essential services including job training, health care, drug/alcohol treatment, childcare and homelessness prevention activities. By helping to support emergency shelter transitional housing and needed support services, Emergency Shelter Grants are designed to move homeless persons toward permanent housing.

Approximately $322 million of the Continuum grants awarded today will fund new and existing programs through *HUD's Shelter Plus Care* program which helps to pay rent and provide permanent housing for disabled homeless individuals and their families. The *Shelter Plus Care* program required that HUD-funded projects help their clients live independently and provide needed supportive services form funding sources other than HUD.

The Goal to End Chronic Homelessness

For nearly four years, HUD has increasingly emphasized the Bush Administration's goal of ending chronic homelessness in its assistance programs. Research indicates that approximately 10 percent of all homeless persons experience long-term or chronic homelessness, or 150,000 people. These studies also find that this hardest-to-serve population utilizes over half of all emergency shelter resources designed to assist homeless individuals and families. By shifting the federal emphasis toward meeting the needs of the most vulnerable homeless persons, more resources become available for those who experience homelessness as a temporary condition. To learn more about chromic homelessness, visit the Internet.

HUD is the nation's housing agency committed to increasing homeownership, particularly among minorities; crating affordable housing opportunities for low-income Americans; and supporting the homeless, elderly, people with disabilities and people living with AIDS. The Department also promotes economic and community development as well as enforces the nation's fair housing laws. More information about HUD and its programs is available on the Internet at www.hud.gov and espanol.hud.gov.

# #

HIGLIGHTS OF HUD'S HOMELESS ASSISTANCE

- Largest total award of Federal funds for homeless assistance in history more than $1.4 billion is being awarded to an unprecedented number of projects nationally, more than 4,400. This is also the fourth consecutive year funding for homeless assistance has increased to record levels.
- 1,089 of the project awards being announced today target individuals experiencing

chronic homelessness. Total funding to these projects will exceed $370 million, a commitment that directly supports the national goal of ending chronic homelessness by 2012.

- Approximately half of all funding announced today, totaling $628 million, is being awarded to more than 1,100 projects that provide permanent housing solutions for homeless persons.
- More than 900 local projects that primarily serve mothers and their children will receive $220 million.
- Approximately 400 shelters that primarily serve victims of domestic violence will receive $92.6 million.
- Nearly $33.8 million is being awarded to 133 projects that primarily target homeless veterans among those they serve.

Chapter Eight 3. Helpful Highlights

<u>Characteristics of Transitional Housing
for Homeless Families</u>

Final Report
Published by the Urban Institute

Introduction

The concept of transitional housing has a long history In the fields of mental health and corrections departments developed these residential programs to ease the transition back into regular housing for people leaving mental hospitals or prisons. Stevens (2005) describes the history of halfway houses for people leaving correctional settings, and their transition quite recently into community residential centers. To use one state as an example, in 1974 Ohio had 22 certified halfway houses for people leaving prison (Ohio Adult Parole Authority 2005). Policy makers in the mental health arenas were also focusing on community-based residential and nonresidential services during the 1970's and early 1980's (Biegel and Naparstek 1982). In 1982 an American Psychiatric Association task force published its report. A *Typology of Community Residential Services* (APA 1984), which sought to establish a common nomenclature for residential programs serving people with serous mental illness located throughout the country. The task force has spent four years identifying, cataloging, and attempting to classify the many such programs in existence at that time.

These community-based transitional programs were developed for many reasons, including a desire to avoid the high cost of institutional versus community-based care and a desire or legal obligation to maintain some intermediate level of supervision over people being released from institutions. One of the historical motivations for developing transitional community residential settings comes closes to the one driving the growth of transitional housing programs for homeless people. Officials running state agencies and institutions saw people fail in the community and return to institutions when they did not have the skills, connections, or supports that would help them establish themselves independently. Transitional programs were developed to increase the likelihood that those released from institutions would, once reinforced by the learning and development acquired during a period in a transitional program, be able to sustain independent living in the community.

Chapter Eight 4. Helpful Highlights

Emergency Shelter Grants (ESG) Program

The Emergency Shelter Grants program provides homeless persons with basic shelter and essential supportive services. It can assist with the operational costs of the shelter facility, and for the administration of the grants. ESG also provides short-term homeless prevention assistance to persons at imminent risk of losing their own housing due to eviction, foreclosure, or utility shutoffs.

Grantees, which are state governments, large cites, urban counties, and U.S. territories, receive ESG grants and make these funds available to eligible recipients, which can be either local government agencies or private nonprofit organizations. The recipient agencies and organizations, which actually run the homeless assistance projects, apply for ESG funds to the governmental grantee, and not directly to HUD. Feel free to view all CPD formula grants, including the ESG grant, or contact your local field office for further assistance.

ESG funds are available for the rehabilitation or remodeling of a building used as a new shelter, operations and maintenance of the facility, essential supportive services (i.e., case management, physical and mental health treatment, substance abuse counseling, childcare, etc.), homeless prevention, and grant administration.

Grantees, except for state governments, must match ESG grant funds dollar for dollar with their own locally generated amounts. These local amounts can come from the grantee oar recipient agency or organization; other federal, state and local grants; and from "in-kind" contributions such as the value of a donated building, supplies and equipment, new staff services, and volunteer time.

For further details please consult the ESG Desk Guide.

Other Resources
- CPD Performance Measurement Website
  The implementation of the outcome performance measurement system and its use by grantees will enable HUD to collect information on the outcomes of activities funded with CPD formula grant assistance.
  - CPD Performance Measurement Outcome System Questions and Answers – Nov 18, 2005
  - Interim Update on Performance Measurement
  - Federal Register Notice

Chapter Eight

5. Helpful Highlights

Subsidized Housing

Apartment buildings

Row houses.

Chapter Eight Helpful Highlights

INCOME LIMIT CHART

1 Person	2 Person	3 Person	4 Person	5 Person	6 Person	
13950	18200	20500	22750	24350	26400	30% of MEDIAN
26550	30350	34150	37590	41000	44000	Very low income
41700	47700	53650	59600	64350	69150	Low Income

When listing income, you must include the following information:

1. All sources of money you or any member of your household receives (wages,
2. welfare, alimony, social security, pension, etc.)
3. Any money you receive on behalf of your children (child support, social security for
4. children, etc.)
5. Income from assets (interest from a savings account, credit union, or certificate of
6. deposit, dividends from stock, etc.)
7. Earnings from second job or part-time job.
8. Any anticipated income (such as a bonus or pay raise you expect to receive).

Chapter 9

Money for Daycares

Thitis chapter will cover the purpose of Daycares, the types of service provided, set-up and licensing regulations, and instructions on how to diversify your nonprofit agency with daycare services.

Purpose of Daycares

The structure of the working family has changed through the years

in the United States. A few decades ago, it was the woman of the house that was responsible for the daily care of the children and the elderly in their families. With the increase of employment with two parent households, it has become necessary for the establishment of more and more daycare facilities for the elderly and for school aged children. In France, Italy, and the Soviet Union, Daycares have always been a part of the public school system. We have a variety of programs that fall up under the daycare label.

Types of Daycare

There are two kinds of daycare services in general. The first kind is set up in the home of the provider. The provider is limited to a small number of clients to care for. The in-home provider of services must also go through a lot of the same licensing procedures that the commercial daycare provider has to endure. The second type is the commercial provider. The number of persons that is cared for depends on the amount of space that is available, and the number of staff. It is important that there is a standard staff-to-client ratio.

Set-Up of Daycare Programs

Starting up a Daycare program for people in your home requires that you contact the city that you plan to start your business in. Each city has standard requirements. Some cities may require that you complete local requirements in order to be eligible. If you do not live in a home that is zoned for mixed-use, then you will be required to get permission from the city commissioner, or the building inspectors, or both. Running a Daycare from your home is considered a business, so the property will have to meet compliance for a business unit as well as a residential property. In some instances this can take months, but you only have to go through it one time. Once you get the occupancy permit for your home daycare, you do not have to reapply.

If you are going to accept vouchers from the county of the state for payment in lieu of private pay, then you must also complete the licensing requirements with the agency that you want to accept vouchers from. The application process is tedious. It may be a good idea to hire a consultant, to move the process along. Also take the time to visit other businesses that are providing the same type of service that you wish to provide.

The compliance requirements are not as stringent for a home-based daycare as they are for a commercial daycare. Most commercial daycares require that you have a licensed teacher on staff, or that your program director have a minimum of a Master's Degree in Education or childcare. Also you will need a dietician to complete the menus for the program. All menus submitted have to be signed by a licensed dietician.

Because program set-up varies slightly from state to stare, we recommend that you contact the county office and the state licensing department to request an application, and review the rules for your state. Expect the process to take approximately six months to a year. The determining factor for gaining approval from the licensing agency is based on how fast you submit all of the licensing requirements. In most states there is a restriction on hiring felons, or if you have a home-based daycare, having felons in the home living there.

Daycare programs are in demand in every state to provide services for children as well as the elderly. If you have a passion for caring for this population, then it is wise to start the certification process early, if you plan on beginning the services soon.

While you are in the process of completing the certification process, and waiting on license, there are safety and health regulations that also have to be adhered to. For instance, the Department of Health and Safety will need to inspect a commercial program for equipment compliance. Food has to be prepared and stored at a certain temperature. There has to be proper ventilation. Also, all toys and other equipment that is offered by your program have to be inspected and approved for safety.

An additional requirement is that the program maintains liability insurance. The insurance is standard, and does not cost that much, but is a good prevention measure. For most programs that are requesting licensure, it is mandatory. For example of an incident that could close your doors without having insurance I the parent that sues you because one of your male students touches a female student that is the same age inappropriately. That is a sexual harassment lawsuit, and without proper handling, could close the doors of your agency quick. Insurance companies have the staff and the attorneys to negotiate those types of incidents so that you can continue to supervise your agency. For about $700 annually, you can receive around a million dollars of liability insurance in case of incident. The price is well worth the benefit when you are caring for a population that cannot care for themselves.

Diversifying your Daycare Program

Many daycare programs are plagued by the long periods between the county payout periods. The county is the entity responsible for mailing out the payments for agencies that accept vouchers. There are many delays. The checks are printed late. The funding is calculated more times late than early, and mostly, county agencies are also awaiting payment. It is a series of never-ending delays. Unfortunately, the mortgage holder, or your employees do not care about the delays. It is all the problem of the director of the program. If an employee is lucky, they are able to hire a few individuals that understand the problems associated with county voucher payments. Unfortunately, more often than not, there is a rapid turnover of employees as a result of employment payment issues. It is not the fault of the director in most instances. The way to combat the problem is to diversify your daycare program. The way to do that is by employing several strategies. The first one is to sublease space out to similar projects. If you have a large space you can legally rent part of the space or offices to other agencies or consultants that are a part of your mission indirectly, or offering similar services. For instance, if there is a consultant that does accounting services for your daycare and others, but does not want to pay the high cost of overhead, they may consider renting a small space of your commercial area to offset the cost of rent. There are hundreds of smaller agencies with solid missions that cannot afford the overhead costs of renting their own office. Neighborhood organizations and also scholastic or agencies specializing in literacy may also be a good candidate to sublease space to.

The second way to diversify your agency is by using the same principle that we recommended for housing programs. Diversify your funding sources is a sure way to offset some of the effects of waiting on county funding to kick in.

One way to do this is to partner with a church at the beginning of your daycare project. Churches have a structure in place that allows them to accept tithes. If you decide to partner with them, set up the agreement that a number of jobs will be filled by church members, creating jobs for the parishioners. Church volunteers are also plentiful when you enter into a viable partnership with a church.

Also, because you have a daycare, why not also implement a mentoring program, a training program, meal-on-wheels, or some other type of service that will compliment your daycare and add several funding sources to the pot of money coming in. If you have the space, consider diversifying your funders.

Vouchers are part of a large bureaucratic system. It is best to have programming that will also add foundations and corporations as funders. If you have a variety of payments coming in monthly, you will eliminate the stress and strain of having to pay employees that may become irate when you have to make an announcement that the checks from the county are late. With a versatile funding base, there will always be a stream to draw from when needed.

If part of your diversification strategies involve elderly programming, that makes available a large pot of funding to you. Many funders on all levels only cater to the elderly. Also, on a federal level, you have the Department of Aging. Further, often a few of the elderly persons in your program may be disabled or retired veterans. That is a separate pot of money.

Going back to the quiz questions in Chapter Three, ask yourself if you multi-task well. If you do, then the sky is the limit. Add as many components to your daycare program as you can comfortably manage, and watch the money pile up!

Chapter 9   Helpful Highlights

   Below displays a partnership between a large church and daycare center, to give the reader an example of the type of funding that can be acquired and the large array of services that can be offered under one business structure.

Today, New Life in Christ Church and Little Angels Day Care Center stand on part of the 11.5 acres the congregation purchased. The community worship center includes a sanctuary, gym, bookstore, snack bar, industrial kitchen, offices and an education and meeting space. Future development plans include a school, family center and housing.

Little Angels Day Care Center is a bright, colorful, interactive and state-certified facility that serves children aged 6 weeks through preschool. In addition, parents of school-aged children can take advantage of a before- and after-school program. Current enrollment at the center is 53 and quickly growing to full capacity of 105 children. While the center offers market-rate child care, it also works with the Children's Home and Aid Society of Illinois to provide free or greatly reduced care to low-income families.

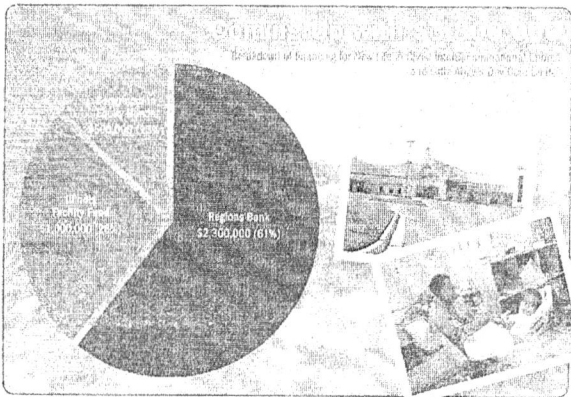

Chapter 10

Money for your state

The future of nonprofits

History is constantly recycling and resurging. The country is entering into a recession. Also we are in the middle of enormous war spending time. It is time to look at the big picture.

Each and every time, immediately after a war ends, social services funding and services become the number one priority. The purpose is to deprogram the nation, and restore the American dream. In the past, some of the most prestigious nonprofit organizations began offering services immediately following wartime. A few of the foundations were Sherwin Williams that universalized commercial and residential paint; the Rockefeller Foundation who specialized in research; and the Ford Foundation that displayed industrialization of the car industry. The time following war indicates as new beginning and a fresh start for the country. History always repeats itself.

This is the time to begin to organize your nonprofit and to start putting your plan into action. If you position yourself now, the money will come.

If you have made a decision to set up your own nonprofit, there is no reason to reinvent the wheel. There are hundreds of nonprofit organizations all over the country. There is a large possibility that your idea has been done already in some form.

What we suggest is to find a nonprofit that has similar components to the services that you wish to offer, and then contact them. Make the contact initially by telephone, and ask if you can make an appointment to come out for a visit. Do not be disappointed if you do not receive the response that you expected. Because there are so many nonprofits, simply hang up and call another one. There are more staff that will be responsive than not.

When you call or visit, make sure that you have composed a list of realistic questions to ask the staff member that you make contact with. A very good question is to ask the staff person to share three main obstacles that they have encountered. This is very important, because it gives you a head start on what to expect.

Chapter 10 Helpful Highlights

The following pages lists nonprofit organizations from 15 states:

1. Arizona
2. District of Columbia
3. Florida
4. Georgia
5. Illinois
6. Kentucky
7. Louisiana
8. Nebraska
9. New York
10. Ohio
11. Oregon
12. Puerto Rico
13. Texas
14. Washington
15. Wyoming

ARIZONA

Name	State
Faith of Our Fathers Radio Ministry	AZ
Young Artists Community Ballet Inc.	AZ
Pacs- Pakistan American Cultural Society	AZ
1010 International Net. Inc.	AZ
12 Steps for Christian Living Center	AZ
161st Air Refueling Wing Minutemen	AZ
18 Society Foundation of Arizona	AZ
180th Field Artillery	AZ
In10 Inc.	AZ
1st United Charitable Trust	AZ
1st Way of Maricopa County	AZ
200312	AZ
21st Century Ministry	AZ
21st Century Music Ministry	AZ
24th Infantry Division Association	AZ
260 Club of Green Valley Inc.	AZ
29th Street Coalition	AZ
390th Memorial Museum Foundation	AZ
3ho Foundation of Arizona, Inc.	AZ
4 H Clubs Yuma County	AZ
4 H Clubs and Affiliated 4 H Organization	AZ
4 Winds Academy Inc.	AZ
4 H Clubs and Affilliated 4-H Desert Equistars	AZ
4 H Clubs and Affilliated 4-H Desert Hills Wranglers	AZ
4 H Clubs and Affilliated 4-H Dog Gone Dewey Wranglers	AZ
4-Winds Academy Inc.	AZ
4th Clubs & Affiliated 4th Cinder Hillbillies	AZ
500 W. Aspinwall	AZ
51st Ave Friendship Center Inc.	AZ

Arizona Cont.

60 Plus Club of Sun Lakes	AZ
7th Avenue Sobriety Inc.	AZ
88 Crime Inc.	AZ
90th Bomb Group Association	AZ

District of Columbia

ASTRA	DC
1	DC
100 Black Men of Greater Washington DC	DC
100 Percent Recycled Paperboard Alliance Inc.	DC
1313 L Street N W Inc.	DC
14th & U Main Street Initiative	DC
14th and U main Str Commercial District Inc.	DC
14th Street Heights Main Street Program	DC
1776 Foundation	DC
18-35 Inc.	DC
1800 Massachusetts Avenue Inc.	DC
1992 Benefit Plan Retiree Health Benefit Reserve Trust	DC
2 M Center Inc.	DC
2002 Friends of the National Zoo	DC
2005 National Conference on Appellate Justice Foundation	DC
2020 Vision Education Fund	DC
2020 Vision National Project	DC
2021 Street Building Corp.	DC
21st Century School Fund	DC
2nd District Religious Education & Charitable Development	DC
50 Years Is Enough Network	DC
555 New Jersey Ave. N.W. Inc.	DC
5801 Foundation, Inc. The	DC
624 South Michigan Avenue Inc.	DC

District of Columbia, Cont.

6th & I Synagogue Inc.	DC
9 11 Public Discourse Project	DC
9/11 Public Discourse Project	DC
A C N M Foundation	DC
A C T Affordable Housing Inc.	DC
A D A N A	DC
A Greater Washington, Inc.	DC
A Harvest Biotech Foundation International	DC
A Phillip Randolph Institute	DC
A Prophets Reward Ministry	DC
A R E Public Charter School Inc.	DC
A Ray of Hope Interdenominational Ministry	DC
A Salon Ltd.	DC
A T I S	DC
AAA Foundation for Traffic Safety	DC
Aa b c Commissioning Group	DC
Aar Nric	DC
AARP	DC
AARP Chapters Group Return	DC

Florida

10th Life Sanctuary Inc.	FL
Loves Haven for Abandoned Pets Inc.	FL
What About You? Inc.	FL
#773 Gulf Coast Council Trust Fund BSA	FL
0550 Community Involvement	FL
1-800-Mass-Times Trust	FL
10 Seconds Inc.	FL
100 Angels Charitable Foundation	FL
100 Black Memorial Of Gtr Ft. Lauderdale	FL

Florida, Cont.

100 Black Men of Jacksonville Inc.	FL
100 Black Men of Pensacola Inc.	FL
100 Black Men of Tampa Bay Inc.	FL
100 Club of Gibsonton	FL
100 Club of South Palm Beach County	FL
100 Deputies 100 Kids Inc.	FL
1000 Friends of Florida, Inc.	FL
101 Club Inc.	FL
1041 United States Power Squadrons Clearwater Sa	FL
10th Life Santuary Inc.	FL
1141 Charitable Foundation, Inc.	FL
12 Who Care Community Services Award	FL
1213 William Str Corp.	FL
12761 Kfc Annunciation Council	FL
128 Place Inc.	FL
1292 Amvets Inc.	FL
13 Bomb Squad Association	FL
13 Ugly Men Inc.	FL
131 University Credit Union	FL
131 University Culture	FL
135 Electrici 29ia State Chartered Cr in Fl	FL
13th Bomb Squadron Association	FL
14 S Palafox Place Inc.	FL
1420 Foundation	FL
14th Air Force Association Inc.	FL
1635 Venetian Isles Chapter City of Hope	FL
17th Airborne Division Association	FL
1904 Foundation Inc.	FL

Georgia

Pace	GA
1	GA
1 Corinthians 13	GA
1 for Life Ministry Inc.	GA
1 for Life Ministry Inc.	GA
10/1 Foundation Inc.	GA
100 Black Men Macon Middle GA Inc.	GA
100 Black Men of America	GA
100 Black Men of Atlanta	GA
100 Black Men of Augusta	GA
100 Black Men of Columbus GA Inc.	GA
100 Black Men of North Metro Atlanta Inc.	GA
100 Black Men of Savannah Inc.	GA
100 Black Men of South Metro Inc.	GA
100 Black Men of West Georgia Inc.	GA
100 North Riverside LLC	GA
100 Spear Street Owners	GA
100 Spear Street Owners Corp.	GA
11 Atlanta Community Services Awards	GA
1201 5400 Corp. dba Rock to the Rescue	GA
1438 Inc.	GA
1440 New York Avenue Corp.	GA
150 Newport Avenue Corp.	GA
151 North Delaware Street	GA
1818 Club Inc.	GA
1876 Defoor Ave. Condominium Assoication Inc.	GA
1st & 8th Support Group Inc.	GA
1st Seniorsolutions Inc.	GA
2 C 9 Foundation, Inc.	GA
2 or 3 Gathered Together Inc.	GA
20 South Clark Street Owners Corp.	GA
200 Club of the Coastal Empire Inc.	GA
2004 U.S. Figure Skating Championships Inc.	GA

Georgia (cont.)

21077 Cartersville	GA
21st Century Partnership of Middle Georgia Inc.	GA
22nd Infantry Regiment Society Inc.	GA
230 John WEsley Dobbs Blvd Ventures Inc.	GA
24 Hour Club of Savannah Inc.	GA
24 Karat Club	GA

Illinois

I AM Temple of Chicago Inc.	IL
#2 MT Pleasant M B Church	IL
Til Healing Comes Ministries	IL
I M P A C T	IL
Society of Plastics Engineers Inc.	IL
05 Great Lakes Region 5 Inc.	IL
10 21 Foundation	IL
10-33 Ambulance Services Limited	IL
100 Black Men Chicago	IL
100 Black Men of Alton Inc.	IL
100 Black Men of Central IL Inc.	IL
100 Black Men of Chicago	IL
100 Club of Grundy County Nfp	IL
100 Treetops Lane Investment Group Lic	IL
11 10 02 Foundation	IL
1117 Electrical Workers Association	IL
112 Education Foundation	IL
117 Elec Workers Association	IL
12 County Employers Coop & Educational Trust	IL
12 South Michigan Preservation Society Inc.	IL
1261 Foundation	IL

Illinois cont.

1311 S Balmoral Condominium Association	IL
1330 Connecticut Avenue Inc.	IL
1330 Connecticut Avenue Land Inc.	IL
1335 Foundation	IL
137 Films Nfp	IL
13th District Order of AHEPA Scholarship Foundation Inc.	IL
150 Monument Inc.	IL
150 Sparks	IL
1500 Chase Corp.	IL
15190 Prestonwood Boulevard Inc.	IL
15th Ward Organization Crime Stoppers	IL
18th & Wabash Corp. D/B/A - The Studios	IL
1923 Fund	IL
1st Sr. Solutions Inc.	IL
1st Way Pregnancy Support Services	IL
2 G Charitable Foundation	IL

Kentucky

We Can- Community Development Corp.	KY
100 Black Men of Louisville Inc.	KY
1000 Missionary Movement	KY
101st Airborne Division Association Inc.	KY
11 11 Inc. Aka New Center for Contemporary Art	KY
11 59 Ministry Inc.	KY
1300 S 3rd Str Block Association Inc.	KY
13th Street Club Inc.	KY
15th District Highland Middle Ptsa	KY
1813 Uaw Local International Union United Aerospace	KY
1893 Education Foundation Corp.	KY

Kentucky cont.

1st Area of Kentucky Auto Workers of America	KY
2007 National Sr. Games Inc.	KY
21c Museum Foundation Inc.	KY
21st Century Parks Inc.	KY
233 West Broadway Building	KY
2nd Cavalry Association	KY
3 4 Cali Chapter 35th Infantry Association	KY
3108 Foundation, Inc.	KY
3rd and 4th Areas of KY Cap Council	KY
4-H Clubs & Affiliated 4-H Adair County 4-H Council	KY
4-H Clubs & Alliliated 4-H Organization	KY
531 inc	KY
5th & 6th Areas of KY Cap Council	KY
828 Foundation	KY
A	KY
A A O N M S- Oleika Temple Shrine Clubs	KY
A A U of Northern Kentucky Inc.	KY
A B Happy Chandler Foundation	KY
A Brighter Future Learning Center	KY
A Choice for Life Inc.	KY
A Helping Hand Adoption Agency Inc.	KY
A Loving Choice Preg Research Center Inc.	KY
A M Yealey Elementary Parent Teacher Organization Inc.	KY
A New Beginning for Women	KY
A New Beginning for Women Cultivating A Rose Inc.	KY
A New Story Foundation Inc.	KY
A Place for United States Development Center Inc.	KY
A Quiet Place Inc.	KY
A Summer Institute for Young Musicians Inc.	KY
A-Optic Inc.	KY

Nebraska

Narovec Scholarship Trust, Verna A.	NE
Nata Board of Certification Inc.	NE
Nathan Ashford Fund Inc.	NE
National Alliance for The Mentally Ill Nebraska Inc.	NE
National Arbor Day Foundation	NE
National Association for Family & Community Education	NE
National Association for Family and Lancaster County	NE
National Association For Family and Mcpherson County	NE
National Association for Family and Phelps County	NE
National Association for Family and Rock County	NE
National Association of Fsc County Nebrask Fsa	NE
National Associaton of Letter Carr Branch 8	NE
National Association of Letter Carriers	NE
Postmasters United States	NE
National Association of Retired Postal Inspectors	NE
National Association Purch Mgr-Cent NE	NE
Natonal Autumn Leaf Collectors Club	NE
National Buffalo Foundation	NE
National Burn Institute	NE
National Collegiate Honors Council	NE
National Congress of Old West Shootists	NE
National Council Negro Women Inc.	NE
National Council of Instructional Admin	NE
National Council of Jewish Women-Omaha Section	NE
National CPA Health Care Advisors Association	NE
National Elec Contractors Assoc. Nebraska Chapter	NE
National Federation of the Blind of Nebraska	NE
National Forage Testing Association Inc.	NE
National Gifted Children's Fund	NE
National Heart Savers Association, Inc.	NE
National Hemophillia Foundation Nebraska Chapter	NE
National Indemnity Co. Employee Benefit Trust	NE
National Kidney Foundation of Nebraska	NE
National League of Postmasters of Nebraska	NE

New York cont.

1026-28 Cauldwell Ave. HDFC	NY
1035 Broadway Housing Development Fund Co Inc.	NY
1039 Boston Road Housing Development Fund Corp.	NY
1040 Kids Inc.	NY
104th Precenct Youth Council	NY
1051 College Ave. HDFC Corp.	NY
1055 College Avenue HDFC Corp.	NY
1056 Equities Inc.	NY
105th Floor Heroes Fund Inc.	NY
107 Linden Str HDFC	NY

OHIO

Ghanaian Foundation Inc.	OH
The Word Childcare Center	OH
#7340 VFW Pvt Chas Gailey Post	OH
ETF Engineers & Technicians of the Future	OH
100 Times Foundation	OH
1000 Friends of Central Ohio	OH
1002 Foundation	OH
102nd Infantry Division Association	OH
103rd Ohio Volunteer Infantry	OH
103rd Ovi Memorial Foundation	OH
1042 VFW	OH
1082 VFW Of the United States	OH
1116 Brookview Inc.	OH
1181 Uaw	OH
11th Hour Theatre Co	OH
1213 Club	OH
12th Armored Division Memorial Museum Foundation Inc.	OH
1313 Opeiv	OH
1347 West Fifth Ave. Corp.	OH
1360 Benevolent & Protective Order of the Elks	OH
14th Str Community Center	OH

Oregon cont.

2 Gyriz Performative Arts Inc.	OR
200312	OR
211 Information	OR
21st Century Community Schoolhouse	OR
21st Century Fund	OR
2828 Corbett Inc.	OR
300 Main Inc.	OR
3d Center of Art and Photography	OR
3e Strategies	OR
4 H Clubs , 4 H Leaders Association	OR
5068 Frat Order of Eagles	OR
5068 Fraternal Order of Eagles	OR
5207 Western Foundation	OR
549 C Unlimited	OR
549 C Unlimited Smiths Booster Club	OR
54th National Square Dance	OR
54th National Square Dance Lee E Ashwi	OR
659 Labor Management Coop	OR
7th Bombardment Group (H) Hist Fund	OR
9-10-11 for Fiscal Responsibility	OR
939th Air Refueling Wing Foundation	OR
A	OR
A & A Scottish Rite Valley of Rosebury	OR
A & A Scottish Rite Valley of Roseburg	OR
A Child's Eye Playhouse	OR
A Child's Place	OR
A Childs Way Kindergarten	OR
A Child's Way Preschool	OR
A E Pronet	OR
A F M and Cad	OR
A Family for Every Child	OR

Oregon cont.

A G C Teamsters Vacation Holiday Trust	OR
A New Song for The Nations	OR
A Non Profit Corp. Myongji-Portland Inc.	OR
A Nonprofit Corp. World Peace Center	OR
A O K Club Inc.	OR
A Phillips Square	OR

Puerto Rico

A & B Debt Management of Puerto Rico Corp.	PR
Academia DE Directores Medicos DE Puerto Rico	PR
Accion Laboral Unitaria Y Defensora Local 2341	PR
Accion Laboral Unitaria Y Defensora Local 2741	PR
Accion Social DE P R Inc.	PR
Acciou Lagoral Unitaria Y Defensora	PR
Adoradores Unidos Inc.	PR
Advance Bilingual School Corp.	PR
Advancer Local Development	PR
Advancer Local Development Corp.	PR
AFGE Local 0055	PR
AFGE Local 2408	PR
Alberque Olimpica DE Puerto Rico Inc.	PR
Albergue El Paraiso Corp.	PR
Alianza Municipal De Servicios	PR
Alianza Municipal DE Servicios Integrados	PR
Alianza Para El Desarrolio DE Puerto Rico Inc.	PR
Alianza Para Un Puerto Rico Sin Drogas Inc.	PR
Alliance for the New Humanity Inc.	PR
Altergarten Las Teresas II	PR

Puerto Rico cont.

Altergarten Las Teresas I Inc.	PR
Altergarten Las Teresas Inc.	PR
American College of Physicians Puerto Rico Chapter	PR
American Federation of Government 2608 AFGE	PR
American Federation of Government Local 2408	PR
American Postal Workers Union	PR
Amigos DE San Jose Inc.	PR
Anaco Education Services Inc.	PR
Andanza Inc.	PR
Angel DE LA Guarda Inc.	PR
Ann Wigmore Natural Health Institute Inc.	PR
APNI Inc.	PR

Texas

Free for Life Animal Sanctuary Corp.	TX
Green Bar Bill Hillcourt Trust	TX
R Association of Rice University	TX
#6984 PTA Texas Congress	TX
(0792) Lockheed Martin Leadership Association	TX
Houston Outreach Task Inc.	TX
04 Arts Foundation	TX
1 Plays Players— Harbour Playhouse	TX
100 Black Men of Metro Houston Inc.	TX
100 Club Inc.	TX
100 Club of Brazoria County	TX
100 Club of Central Texas Inc.	TX
100 Club of Jefferson & Hardin County	TX
100 Club of Wharton County Inc.	TX
100 Club, Inc. The	TX
1000 Hills Ministry International	TX

Texas cont.

101 Veterans Inc.	TX
1030 Executive Building Inc.	TX
1100 Meredith Lane Inc.	TX
11095 Viking Inc.	TX
116 Aerie Frtl Order of Eagles	TX
11th Street Bingo Association	TX
12 Harmony Club of Amarillo Inc.	TX
121 Community Outreach Inc.	TX
123 Divorce Company	TX
136th Silber Eagles Inc.	TX
1394 High Performance Serial Bus Trade Association	TX
15 57 Ministry	TX
15:57 Ministry Inc.	TX
1747 Luther Jones Elementary	TX
17th District Dental Society	TX
180 House Inc.	TX
1894 Inc.	TX

Washington

$ Fraternal Order of Eagles 4225	WA
10 99 Foundation	WA
1000 Friends of Washington	WA
10000 Years Institute	WA
101 Club Washington Athletic Club	WA
1201 Kas Inc.	WA
13th Regional Heritage Foundation	WA
1414 Club	WA
1416 Association	WA
1419 Association	WA
1501 Piano Road Inc.	WA
1st Choice Pregnancy Care Center	WA

Washington

1st Way of Moses Lake	WA
21st Century Basic Human Services	WA
21st Century Cardiac Surgical Society Inc.	WA
21st Century Fund	WA
21 Street Foundation	WA
2205 Club	WA
26a Washington Corporation	WA
2v/Act	WA
3 G Harvest	WA
33 Fainting Spells	WA
390th Bomg Vet Association	WA
3g Harvest	WA
4-H Clubs & Affiliated 4-H	WA
4-H International Programs Committee	WA
444S Foundation	WA
4470505 Greater Richland Little League	WA
4782 St. Josep 29 IA Knights of Columbus	WA
4985 American Federation of Techers	WA
4p - Support Group	WA
598 Building Association Inc.	WA
59th Fighter Squadron	WA

Wyoming

12-24 Club Inc.	WY
1814 Weeks Avenue HDFC	WY
4-H Clubs Teton County	WY
801 Bishop P A Mcgovern Knights of Columbus	WY
90th Security Forces Top 4	WY
A A O N M S Kalif Temple Group Return	WY
A Career in Energy Inc.	WY
A D O P P T Inc.	WY

Wyoming

A Process of Collaboration A Circle of	WY
Aaonms & Affliates-Kalif Temple	WY
Abate Substance Abuse Project	WY
Abbas House	WY
Absaroka Inc.	WY
Access Home Inc.	WY
Access Tours Inc.	WY
Accredited Debt Counseling Inc.	WY
Actors Mission	WY
Adventures in Christian Kamping	WY
Adventures in Kamping	WY
Adventures Plus Archery Inc.	WY
Advocacy & Resource Center	WY
Advocacy for Visual Arts Inc.	WY
AFL-CIO WY Big Trades	WY
Africa Rainforest & River Conservation Inc.	WY
Agape Foundation	WY
Agnes S Greisen Scholarship Trust	WY
AIA Wyoming A Chapter	WY
The American Institute of Architects	WY
Airport Golf Club Inc.	WY
Albany Co Foster Parent	WY
Albany Co Public Library Foundation	WY
Albany County Association for Retarded Children	WY

Glossary of Terms

Adjusted net income – income left over after deducting expenses.

Advanced ruling – a written letter treating and identifying an agency as a public charity for a five year period, following your date of formation.

Affiliated – created by or closely related or controlled by the same unit.

Audit- to examine, verify, or correct records.

Authorized representative – by submitting Form 2848, an attorney or certified public accountant who is permitted to represent you filing your application for tax-exempt status.

Award – money or check to nonprofit organization.

Award letter – notification of payment with amount of money listed and the arrival date.

Bingo – a game of chance that is gambling.

Business relationships – employment and contractual relationships, or ownership of more than 35% in common.

Bylaws – The internal rules and regulations of an organization.

Certification of filing – articles of incorporation for your organization showing evidence of date and state filed in certificate form.

Charitable trust – gives money to the needy. Interchangeable word with endowment and foundation.

Close connection – a relationship between organizations with usually one person exercising influence over all of the organizations.

Common Control – one or more other organizations that have shared board members.

Community – the local or regional geographic area to be served by an organization.

Community foundation – has support from many donors and are located in a specific community or region.

Compensation – all forms of income and bonuses.

Conflict of interest policy – a policy regulating payments or benefits to authority figures of your agency to avoid mismanagement.

Controlled by disqualified persons – a disqualified person cannot control more than 50% of the total voting power of your agency.

Corporation – an entity organized under Federal or State statute. Also a type of nonprofit funder comprised of a group of people acting as one body or entity.

Definitive Ruling – a written letter from IRS classifying you as a public charity. Can also be issued at the end of the five year advance ruling period.

Develop – the planning, financing, construction, or provision of similar services.

Director – a member of a board of persons who control or govern the Board affairs of an institution or corporation.

Disqualified person – any person that is:
a.   a large contributor
b.   an administrator who has similar powers or responsibilities
c.   person who owns more than 20% of the voting power that is contributed to you
d.   an individual with more than 20% of profits coming to you
e.   a person who owns more than 20% of a trust or estate that is paid to you
f.   a member of the family of any person described above
g.   a corporation in which any person described above hold more than 35% of the total combined voting power.
h.   A trust or estate in which persons described above hold more that 35% of the beneficial interests, and
i.   a partnership in which any individuals described above hold more than 35% of the profits interest.

Donor – one who contributes money to a cause or fund.

Double Dipping – an unethical practice of requesting two or more funders to support the same budget item.

Earmark – donations given to you to assist particular projects.

Economic development – organizations formed to combat deterioration in communities.

Elderly housing – special housing to accommodate the elderly as a class. Elderly is defined as age 62 and older.

Endowment – funds donated, as a source of agency income.

Fair market value – the price that property is valued or sold, having reasonable knowledge of relevant facts.

Family – a persons spouse, ancestors and all siblings, whether whole or half blood.

Financial statement – prepared by auditor or accountant, having special reference to agency spending, assets, and worth.

Fiscal Manager – handles the monetary activities of the agency, such as payroll and paying taxes.

For Profit – a business where revenues are greater than expenses.

Foundation – funds for support of an institution, such as a hospital or school, an endowment established by wealthy families.

Foundation Manager – managing funding, as part of a foundation.

Fundraising – the organized activity of raising funds, whether by volunteers, employees, or paid independent contractors.

Gaming – activities such as bingo, Beano, lotteries, pull tabs, betting, calculator wagering, pickle jars, punch boards, tip boards, tip jars, certain video games, 21, raffles, Keno, split-the-pot, and other games of chance.

Grant – to bestow as an act or privilege, an amount of money given by a funder to a nonprofit agency or corporation primilarily.

Grantee – One to whom a grant is made, the organization that receives the money from a funder.

Grantor – one who makes a grant, the one who gives out the money.

Grassroot agency – a basic organization that is starting from the bottom and providing services.

Gross investment income – gross amount of income from interest and dividends payments.

Gross receipts – monies earned from activities related to your charitable defined activities.

Handicapped – persons with physical or mental disabilities with special needs.

Independent contractors – persons who are not treated as employees. Responsible for paying their own taxes and employee benefits.

Influence legislation – contacting members of a legislative body to propose, support, or oppose legislation.

Intellectual property – property distinct from real or personal property, such as: (a) patents, (b) copyrights (c) trade names (d) formulas and trade secrets.

In the Red – an agency that has more expenses than income. There bottom line will show a negative balance.

Joint ventures – when parties jointly undertake a transaction for mutual profit.

Low-income housing – rental or ownership housing provided to person based on financial need. Development Corporations specialize in this component.

Manage – means to direct or administer.

Mission statement – a public statement of agency objective, usually one full sentence.

Non-fixed payments – payment that is performance based, at the discretion of the funder.

Nonprofit – an agency offering services or similar, usually to a group of people underserved, not for a profit.

990 – tax forms used to file exempt organizations spending annually.

Organizing document – the organizing document determines the type of organizational legal structure.

Per Diem – an amount given for a unit. Per Diem cost could also mean the break down of cost per person to provide a service.

Political – if you promote or oppose through political literature, brochures, pamphlets, or hosting events. Debates and non partisan voter education are not considered political.

Predecessor – an agency whose activities or assets were taken over by another organization.

Private foundation – a 501(C) (3) foundation that does not have a broad range of financial support from the general public.

Program Manager – supervises an aspect of an organization, and reports to administrative staff, such as the director of an agency.

Program report – required to report information gathered during a specified period of time, generally due monthly, depending on funding source.

Program statement – an affirmation of program objectives(s).

Proposal – a plan that is proposed, such as a grant proposal. The word proposal is interchanged with the word grant.

Public charity – an organization that has broad financial support from the general public.

Reasonable compensation – the amount that would ordinarily be paid for like services by similar organizations.

RFP – means Request for Proposal. Usually a meeting, facilitated by funders to give agencies the rules for each grant and allow interactive questions.

Revenue – revenue means gross revenue amounts.

SS-4 – application for Employer Identification Number.

School – a school is an educational organization that maintains a regular faculty, curriculum and students.

Substantial contributor – any person or organization that gave more than $5000.

Successor – an organization that took over or was converted to the current nonprofit status.

Trust – formed through a will or by a trust agreement.

Trustee – member of a board elected or appointed to direct the funds and policy of an institution.

Unusual grants – are unexpected and received from unrelated party, but substantial.

Websites/Resources

Reference

www.clevelandfoundation.com	Chapter 5
Encyclopedia Britannica	Chapter 1
www.foundationcenter.org	Chapter 2 & 5
Foundation Directory	Chapter 10
www.hud.gov	Chapter 8
www.IRS.gov	Chapter 4, 6
www.Jennifer BrunnerOhioSecretary of state.gov	Chapter 5
www.JohnGlennInstitute.org	Chapter 7
www.LittleAngelsDaycarecenter.org	Chapter 9
www.urbaninstitute.org	Chapter 9
www.whitehouse.gov	Chapter 7, 10

Helpful Information

1). 5 Locations of the Foundation Centers in America:

The Foundation Center
Kent H. Smith Library
Floor
1422 Euclid, Suite 1356
Cleveland, Ohio 44115

The Foundation Center
79 Fifth Avenue 2nd
New York, NY 10003
212-620-4230

The Foundation Center
312 Sutter St. Rm 312
San Francisco, CA 94103

The Foundation Center
Hurt Building Suite 150
50 Hurt Plaza
Atlanta, GA 30303

The Foundation Center
1001 Connecticut Avenue NW
Washington, DC 20036

2). U.S. Small Business Administration
    800-827-5722
    www.sbaonline.sba.gov

3). Business Plans for Small Business
    SBA Publications
    P.O. Box 4651
    Denver, CO 80201-0031

4). U.S. Department of Housing & Urban Development
    451 7th St. S.W.
    Washington, DC 20410
    espanol.hud.gov

Index

A

Accountability; *174*
Aging, Department of; *190, 237*
Agriculture, Department of; *19, 185*
AIDS; *32, 183, 205, 207, 213, 215, 216, 222*
Angel Tree; *176*
Annual Campaign Figures; *158*
Annual Campaigns; *8*
Articles of Incorporation; *91, 107*

B

BINGO; *177*
Black Tie Events; *8*
Board of Directors; *136, 153, 154, 156, 166, 176, 177, 178*
Britton, Rev. Charles; *166, 169*
Budget narrative; *126*
Budget, non-profit; *8, 126, 134, 139, 143, 159*
Budget, profit corp.; *8, 126, 134, 139, 143, 159*
Bush, G.W.; *21, 41, 63, 160, 163, 165, 166, 169, 170, 172, 219, 221*

C

Campbell, Commissioner Jane; *186*
Campbell, Mayor Jane; *186*
Carnegie Foundation; *13*
Center for Faith-Based and Community Initiatives; *171*
Chaplain; *188*
Chronicle of Philanthropy; *202*

Church, characteristics; *12, 164, 174, 180, 189, 236*
Churches; *163, 164, 166, 167, 169, 174, 175, 236*
Cleveland Foundation; *21, 38, 46, 133*
Cleveland Ohio; *209*
Clinton administration; *202*
Clinton, William; *21, 84, 172, 202*
Commonwealth Fund; *13, 43*
Community Affairs Department; *168*
Community Reinvestment Act (CRA); *167*
Continuum of Care; *219, 220*

D

DBA (Doing business as); *166*
Department of Health and Safety; *187, 234*
Department of Justice; *22, 23, 127*
Department of Labor; *19, 171, 172*
Dimora, County Commissioner; *186*
Diversity; *189, 190*

E

Economic development; *262*
Education, Department of; *13, 19, 20, 22, 24, 39, 170, 180, 233*
EIN (Employment Identification Number); *8, 100, 101, 102, 117, 119, 121*
EIN form; *8, 117*
Elderly; *190, 210, 262*
Emergency shelters; *191, 196*

Employment and Training Administration; *172*

Equipment, nonprofit; *61, 62, 137*

Evaluation, grant; *8, 126, 130*

Executive Director; *23, 104, 127, 173, 176*

Executive Summary, grant; *126, 127*

F

Faith-based Initiative; *167, 168, 169, 170*

FAQ (Frequently Asked Questions); *123*

Federal grants; *193*

Fellowships; *25, 56, 57*

Felons; *176, 177*

Felons, college; *176, 177*

FHA (Federal Housing Administration); *208*

Financial Statements; *140*

Ford Foundation; *13, 27, 28, 36, 63, 160, 239*

Foundation Center; *14, 15, 16, 17, 18, 269*

G

Grantees; *226, 227*

Grant initiatives; *202*

Grants; *7, 9, 28, 55, 124, 174, 213, 215, 220, 221, 226*

Griffin, Nora Thomas; *205*

H

Halfway houses; *198*

HFTH(Horizons for the Homeless); *205, 206, 207*

Hitchcock Center for Women; *201, 205*

Homeland Security Fund; *170*

Homelessness; *221*

Housing; *9, 19, 20, 25, 67, 168, 170, 180, 183, 190, 191, 193, 195, 200, 203, 204, 208, 213, 214, 215, 218, 224*

Housing and Urban Development(HUD); *19, 20, 67, 170, 193, 214, 218*

Housing Energy Assistance Program(HEAP); *25*

I

invoice; *135, 136, 137*

IRS Form 1023; *82*

J

J; *42, 64, 84, 87, 89, 161, 166, 172, 175*

Job descriptions; *140*

John D. and Katherine T. MacArthur Foundation; *13*

John Simon Guggenheim Memorial Foundation; *13*

Justice Affairs, County; *23*

K

Kellogg, W.K. Foundation; *13, 34, 36*

Kennedy, Fair housing; *20, 21*

Kennedy, John F.; *20, 21*

L

Lesko, Matthew; *58*

Literacy Centers; *24*

Low Income; *229*

M

Mayes, Paula; *23, 24*

Mental Health Agencies; *185*

Methodology, grant; *126, 128*

Metropolitan Housing Authority; *195, 203, 204*

N

Neighborhood; *236*

New York Life Insurance Company; *203*

Nora Thomas-Griffin; *205*

O

Objectives, grant; *126, 129*
ODADAS; *201*
Ohio funding; *194*
Our Place; *124, 176*

P

Peabody Education Fund; *13*
Pew Memorial Trust; *13*
Poverty; *192*
Prison; *2, 176*
Prison Fellowship Program; *176*
Progressive Baptist Church; *164*
Proposal; *23, 67, 265*

Q

Questionnaire; *131*
Quiz; *8, 65, 66, 79*

R

Rehabilitation and Correction; *185*
Resumes; *140*
Robert Wood Johnson Foundation;
    13, 36, 63, 161
Rockefeller Center; *31*
Rockefeller Foundation; *13, 30, 31,
    34, 37, 63, 161, 239*
Rockefeller, J.D.; *13, 15, 30, 31, 34, 37,
    42, 63, 83, 160, 161, 239*
Russell Saga Foundation; *13*

S

Scholarships; *24, 56, 57, 58*
Secretary of State; *19, 82, 89, 90, 91,
    102, 107, 117, 140*
Section 8; *201, 204, 205, 206*
Self-sufficiency; *207*
Shelter; *9, 197, 206, 207, 208, 213,
    215, 220, 221, 226*
Smithsonian Institution; *13*
SRO(Single Residence Occupancy);
    205, 206

Staffing; *197*
State licensure; *186*
Storefronts; *212*
Subsidized housing; *9, 203*
Sustainability; *126, 132*

T

Temporary housing; *200*
Tithes; *174*
Transitional housing; *9, 191, 201*
Turner, Sheila; *24*

U

United States; *15, 18, 19, 20, 27, 32,
    33, 34, 70, 84, 89, 107, 121, 173,
    190, 196, 231*
United Way; *54, 67, 70, 124, 130*
U.S. Marshalls; *200*

V

Veterans;
Volunteers;

W

Wendy's Restaurant; *175*
Williams, Jim; *5, 168, 208, 239*
World War II; *12, 20*
Wrap-around services;

Y

Youth; *21, 22, 23, 63, 160, 172, 181*
Youth Development Initiative; *21,
    22, 23*
Youth Mentoring programs;

ORDER FORM

World Books Etc.

244 West Glendale Avenue, Bedford, Ohio 44146

worldbooks_etc@yahoo.com

Name: _____

Address: _____

City/State: _____

Zip: _____

Title: **FREE MONEY IN AMERICA**

Trade paperback	$19.95
Hardcover	24.95
Shipping/Handling	4.05

How many books? _____ Total $ _____

Forms of Payment Accepted:

Bank checks, money orders, or gift certificates from our company.

Order by U.S. Mail from Above address, or:

By phone: 1-888-384-8776 (or) 1-440-232-7260

Online at Amazon.com, Barnes & Noble.com, and all other online book stores.

ORDER FORM
World Books Etc.
244 West Glendale Avenue, Bedford, Ohio 44146
worldbooks_etc@yahoo.com

Name: _____

Address: _____

City/State: _____

Zip: _____

Title: **FREE MONEY IN AMERICA**

Trade paperback		$19.95
Hardcover		24.95
Shipping/Handling		4.05
How many books? _____	Total $ _____

Forms of Payment Accepted:
Bank checks, money orders, or gift certificates from our
company.

Order by U.S. Mail from Above address, or:
By phone: 1-888-384-8776 (or) 1-440-232-7260

Online at Amazon.com, Barnes & Noble.com,
and all other online book stores.

GRANT MONEY
in America

Book 2 of the Money Series
is coming soon

Features:
- Step-by-Step Instruction on Grant Writing
- Review Sample grants

Also, register for our Correspondence Course on Grantwriting today!

- 22 interactive lessons
- Easy to understand
- Complete at your own pace

For more information, or to register, write the address below:

By Rhonda Turpin

Published by: World Books Etc.
                   244 West Glendale
                   Bedford, Ohio 44146

www.ingramcontent.com/pod-product-compliance
Lightning Source LLC
Chambersburg PA
CBHW020243290326
41930CB00038B/232